A Workbook in

PROGRAM DESIGN

For Public Managers

Leonard I. Ruchelman

State University of New York Press
Albany

Dedicated to Lauren and Zischa and their progeny

Published by
State University of New York Press, Albany

© 1985 State University of New York

Printed in the United States of America

For information, address State University of New York
Press, State University Plaza, Albany, N.Y., 12246

Library of Congress Cataloging in Publication Data

Ruchelman, Leonard I., 1933—
    A workbook in program design for public managers.
     1. Public administration—Cost effectiveness.
2. Public administration—Planning. 3. Problem
solving. 4. Organizational change. I. Title.
JF1411.R83   1985   350.007'2   85-9936
ISBN 0-88706-025-0 (pbk.)

CONTENTS

PREFACE _____

Because public programs are often poorly designed, with little or no thought given to considerations of cost, feasibility, or effectiveness, government and non-profit agencies have unfortunately defaulted on many good ideas. This has been evident in all areas of public service. Billions of dollars and many more man-hours of effort expended over the past decade have barely made a dent on the high crime rate, drug and alcohol abuse, low reading scores, and urban blight, to name some of the more prominent concerns.

Underlying this, is that persons who administer public programs typically have little or no understanding of how to respond to changing needs, especially where new knowledge and different ways of doing things are required. Thus, there tends to be a persisting gap between what is needed and what is achieved. The intent of the present work is to begin to fill this gap by synthesizing what is known about program planning as a body of knowledge, with the application of programs under real life conditions. Most important here is the idea that successful programs usually don't just happen, no matter how desirable, unless a conscious and systematic effort is made to bring them about.

In attempting to demonstrate how one may go about doing a program design project, I have used material from a variety of sources including studies, reports, books, and government manuals. As such, the present work reflects the ideas and experiences of many knowledgeable individuals, both scholars and practitioners. Much remains to be done, however, in testing and further refining the methods of program design. At best, this workbook is but a beginning effort.

I wish to acknowledge the special contributions of my graduate students in urban management, most of whom were also agency practitioners. Through class projects, they helped to test and refine various aspects of the text when in manuscript form. Their support and endorsement has made this effort worthwhile. Hopefully it will also be of use to a wider audience of policy makers, program managers and citizens.

Leonard I. Ruchelman
Old Dominion University
Norfolk, Virginia

CHAPTER 1

INTRODUCTION _____

Typically, pressure for reform begins to mount when funds become scarce or when existing practices become clearly inadequate. Taxpayer resistance, the growing financial problems of communities, and federal cutbacks are giving impetus to the search for new and less costly methods of dealing with the problems of society. An oft-heard theme is that more imaginative and productive approaches in the delivery of services will allow organizations to maintain and improve the quality of services even as resources decline. Though this may appear to stretch credibility, how well organizations approximate this goal is a challenge that can no longer be ignored.

Not only is there the need to improve the management of public programs, but there is also the need to focus more systematically on the planning and organizing of public programs. Because service agencies have been inclined to adopt new programs or change old ones on the basis of instinct or 'gut' feelings, the record of achievement leaves much to be desired.

This, then, is the justification of the present work which focuses on program design from a 'how-to-do-it' perspective. The underlying premise is that an explication of the various elements to be considered in the course of designing or redesigning programs would be a useful and constructive way of assisting public service managers. It is based on the belief that more cost-effective programs are necessary if we are to deal with the increasing complexity and interdependencies of the future, and that we have the knowledge and skills to achieve this. However, the difficulties and obstacles in the way of establishing such programs must also be carefully considered.

WHAT IS PROGRAM DESIGN?

A program can be defined as a plan of action to secure certain objectives; program design is the making of such a plan. It's like going on a journey. Knowing where you want to go, you must plan how to get there. Where the destination is quite distant, involving long travel over difficult terrain, more planning is required than where the destination is nearby. Similarly, more planning is required where two or three destinations have been identified for the journey rather than just one.

Viewed as a whole, a program can be conceived of as a system in which each element is dependent on the other. Program design involves the identification of those elements and properly relating them to each other so that they become mutually supportive. A schedule must be made up and support personnel and facilities should be designated along the way. Using the illustration of a journey, unless sufficient funding is provided, transportation may not be adequate and stopovers may be inconvenient. A breakdown in any of the early stages will affect the flow of activities in the later stages. If the journey is to be successful, as many aspects as possible must be anticipated and provided for in advance.

Programs are of many different kinds covering almost all phases of human existence—from prenatal clinics to services for the elderly, from garbage collection to public safety. Not only do they range over many different fields, but they also vary in size, complexity and duration. It is much more difficult to design a neighborhood development program which would require a diversity of methods and objectives over an extended period of time than to design a small program of limited duration with a specific set of objectives as, for example, a new eighth grade math curriculum to be offered as a summer program.

For those persons who wish to undertake a program design project, the following aspects should be kept in mind. They determine the kind of effort to be exacted, including resources to be utilized and methods and strategies of carrying it out.[1]

Scope. A program may cover the nation, a state, a region, a city or a neighborhood. It may even be limited to one particular site like a school or a hospital. Some programs may operate in scattered locations like an outreach program for drug addicts which utilizes multiple treatment centers in different neighborhoods.

Size. A program may serve a few persons (e.g., remedial reading for college-bound high school students), or it may be applied to hundreds, thousands, or millions of people (e.g., medicare).

Complexity. Some programs are based on very specific objectives (e.g., increase the response time of police patrol cars), while others are more complicated in what they are trying to achieve (e.g., improve the quality of public school education).

Duration. A program may last for only a few hours (e.g., a fund-raising solicitation), a few months, a few years, or continue indefinitely into the future (e.g., a Girl Scout program).

Components. Some program components are clearly identifiable and easy to describe such as when a particular method or a specific technology is being used (e.g., the installation of new smoke detectors or establishing fire drill procedures). Other program components are more diffuse and variable requiring intricate organizational arrangements (e.g., coordinating a regional employment program).

Innovativeness. A program may represent a drastic change from established practices as perceived by management and staff, or, at the other extreme, it may represent only a slight modification or no change at all. This feature is an important consideration in doing program design and is elaborated upon below.

PROGRAM DESIGN AS PLANNED CHANGE

In contrast to unplanned, evolutionary change that occurs without deliberate guidance, program design is a planned or purposive attempt to change the existing way of doing things in an organization. The intent is to modify organization performance in response to a new definition of a situation. For example, a reduction in funding support for an agency or an influx of new clients with special needs may cause the organization membership to rethink the established pattern of providing services and consider some form of program change.

Planned change is closely related to innovation.[2] An innovation is any idea, practice or material artifact perceived to be new by the unit of adoption. In program design, innovation is represented by the search for new ways of enhancing service effectiveness and efficiency. The search usually focuses on identifying ideas that will allow an agency to provide either improved services at the same cost or the same services at lower costs.

It should be noted, however, that while all innovations imply program change, not all program change involves innovation. This is because not everything an organization adopts is perceived as being new. To illustrate, a department of water supply may decide to adopt a computer model for water quality planning. Since this technology was never used before, it is an innovation. The adoption of a computer model also involves change since department personnel who use it must learn how to carry out their roles. Should the agency subsequently decide to abandon the computer system, department personnel would be involved in change, but not innovation.

Types of Program Change

In the public sector, proposals for planned change can usually be classified into three broad programmatic categories, depending upon the type of device or approach that is involved. They are technological change, managerial change, and client-oriented change.[3] These three types are equally applicable for public agencies, voluntary agencies, and for service programs conducted by the private sector.

Technological change refers to the proposed adoption and utilization of a technical device or process such as a machine, a chemical, or a data processing system. Examples in public services are a microcomputer for social data analysis, a nutritional product for persons with special health needs, 'slippery water' for fire-fighting, or hydraulic lifts on motor vehicles for the handicapped. Since the 1960s, the federal government has been trying to stimulate the transfer of technology from private industry, universities and other sources to cities and states. Efforts of the Urban Observatory and HUD User Programs of the Department of Housing and Urban Development, Health and Human Services Clearinghouse programs, and the Commerce Department's National Technical Information Service have shown mixed results. Some cities have reached out on their own to explore the potential for technology utilization. New York, for example, retained the Rand Corporation to provide expert advice. Such efforts have been sporadic, however, with only limited success.

Managerial change refers to the introduction of administrative methods likely to improve organization performance. Examples are team building among personnel, flex-time in designing work schedules, special training or the use of 'quality circles' (i.e., voluntary alternating groups of workers and managers) to address particular problems. An emerging theme which underlies such efforts is productivity improvement. Productivity is based on the relationship between inputs and outputs, measured most commonly in terms of output per man-hour. Programs which aim to increase productivity are being heralded as the means by which public and private organizations can escape the fiscal pressures caused by steadily rising expenditures and less rapidly rising revenues.

Client-oriented change refers to programs where the consumers of a service are provided with some role in the performance of a service. Methods of achieving this include the use of clients as paraprofessional administrators, the use of self-help groups, group decision making, or the establishment of client-elected governing boards.[4] Boston has experimented with Little City Halls as a method of assuring citizen accessibility, and New York City has instituted neighborhood service districts. The underlying rationale to such activities is that they improve bureaucratic performance and provide some assurance of government accountability to local citizens. Here again the results are mixed and more time is needed for assessing the efficacy of such arrangements.[5]

APPROACHES FOR UNDERSTANDING THE PROCESS OF PROGRAM CHANGE

A basic problem in any discussion of program change is that our knowledge of the subject is as yet incomplete, particularly when analysed in the context of planning public programs. Research in this area is relatively new and has not been sufficiently developed for either identifying or explaining the full range of factors that facilitate or impede program change in social systems. Nevertheless, a good deal has been learned about the change process in organizations to justify a review of two basic approaches. The first approach or model focuses on rational problem-solving, and the second deals with organizational change.

Rational Problem-Solving

This approach views program change as rational decision making for the solution of societal problems. In his description of problem solving, the noted philosopher John Dewey distinguished five stages.[6] These are: (1) the recognition of a problem; (2) the definition and clarification of the problem; (3) the production of possible solutions; (4) reasoning through the implications of the solutions; and (5) further observation and experiment leading to acceptance or rejection of the solutions. Though Dewey recognized that this process is an oversimplification and that thinking is too complex to be so well-ordered, it can nevertheless be helpful in dealing with complex situations in public life.

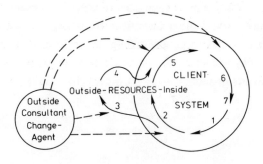

1. NEED FELT
2. PROBLEM DIAGNOSIS
3. SEARCH
4. RETRIEVAL
5. FABRICATION OF SOLUTION
6. APPLICATION
7. EVALUATION

Figure 1.1. The Problem-Solver Model.

SOURCE: Adapted from Ronald G. Havelock, *Innovations in Education: Strategies and Tactics.* Ann Arbor: Center for Research on Utilization of Scientific Knowledge, University of Michigan, 1971, p. 11.

Figure 1.1 represents a refinement of the Dewey model as developed by Ronald G. Havelock.[7] Here the organization (1) recognizes a need for change; (2) defines the problem in light of this need; (3) undertakes either an internal or external search for a solution; (4) identifies different possible solutions as program alternatives; (5) selects an alternative likely to solve the problem; and (6) applies the alternative. The sixth stage leads to a reduction of the original need if the solution is right. If it is not right, as determined through an evaluation, then presumably the first stage is reinitiated and the cycle is repeated until a solution which is truly need-reducing is discovered.

As Figure 1.1 shows, an outside change agent may assist this process by providing ideas specific to the diagnosis or by providing guidance at any or all of the indicated stages. The emphasis, however, is on the organization's own initiative and understanding of the problem and solution and on a reliance on internal rather than external resources. The more these conditions prevail, the more likely that the change effort will succeed.

Though this approach appears to be useful in mapping out the stages for conducting a program design project, certain problems exist which should be recognized. For one, organizations are continually changing and it may be difficult to link such change to program change. Second, the mere adoption of a proposed change by no means assures an effective change effort, for the change object can whither away or evolve into something else in the process of its implementation. The rational problem-solving approach does not account for such factors.

Another limitation is that rational problem-solving does not deal with various bureaucratic factors that can facilitate or impede the implementation of change in organizations. This is particularly critical in the public sector where profit-loss criteria for assessing performance don't usually apply. For example, because public bureaucracies usually do not seek profits as an incentive, and if other incentives are weak, it is not likely that program change will be supported. In addition, the strong compulsion of bureaucracies for self-preservation means that they will tend to favor certain types of proposals, e.g., those that will justify larger annual budgets or more staff, over others that could threaten growth or survival.

Organizational Change

This approach focuses on events within organizations as they undergo change over time. Here program change is viewed as one important aspect of organizational change and is traced through four stages as follows:[8]

(1) Preadoption. This stage extends from the time someone in the community or organization becomes aware of a need for change to the time when a program change is placed on the official agenda for adoption. A basic feature of the preadoption process is setting the agenda of problems to be considered and then testing different possible solutions as to their feasibility. Local agencies are continually faced with many different kinds of problems related to service deficiencies, e.g., lack of community-based programs to serve newly deinstitutionalized patients or disabled clients, declining educational achievement in the schools, or a rising crime rate. At the same time, intermediary organizations such as professional associations, health and welfare councils, consulting groups, and federal and state agencies that have identified an array of possible solutions, attempt to communicate these to the relevant persons. Where communication is successful, decision makers (including practitioners) must then decide on the extent to which the proposed solutions match their priorities. Where problems are many, this is difficult to do. For example, what problems should be given highest priority? How should the local decision maker determine what types of solutions are appropriate? If the proposed solutions are to be seriously considered, decision makers must have an opportunity to test them; and they usually require some evidence that the proposed change was found to be successful in other jurisdictions. Program design occurs in this stage; but, as we shall see, it tries to anticipate the subsequent stages.

(2) Adoption. Adoption can be defined as a decision to allocate scarce local resources to a program change. Usually, such resources are financial, though commitments in manpower or legal authorization such as the granting of a license are other examples. According to W. Henry Lambright, the decision to adopt usually requires a search that yields a variety of solutions. Sometimes small-scale pilot tests are made of the more innovative proposals. At other times consultants are used. The particular approach depends upon the degree of innovativeness involved as well as the nature of the problem. From this may emerge the formal adoption of a specific program change or, just as easily, a rejection of it. Thus, adoption is viewed as part of a complex process involving many smaller decisions that lead to it. Problems and solutions are gradually better defined and linked over time. Research has shown that attempts to match particular solutions to problems work better under the following conditions:

—When the adopting agency has a professional staff, is less formally organized, and is decentralized;

—When the change object has a perceived relative advantage over and is less complex than other proposals or the status quo, is compatible with the adoption agency, and is easy to communicate;

—When the use of the change object is supported by officials, opinion leaders and practitioners in the adopting agency.

(3) Implementation. A program change that is adopted must be implemented. During this phase, the administering agency tests the chosen solution under actual operating conditions and decisions are made to either continue, modify or reject it. The program change may be abandoned at this stage because of better knowledge as to what it can and cannot do; or it may be terminated because other actors, some of whom are external to the community, withdraw their subsidy. If local response to the change is favorable, however, local support may be so great that it will become needed rather than merely nice to have; and what is needed will be funded by local sources, irrespective of funding policies external to the community.

Prior to the 1970s, implementation was seen as a technical, nonpolitical set of activities that evolved in response to directives from decision makers at the top of the political-administrative hierarchy; administrators were viewed as neutral implementors. Now it is recognized that various participants who have a stake in the outcome continue to negotiate with each other during the course of implementing a program. This includes administrators in addition to such other contenders as interest groups, political parties, elected officials, the mass media and clients. Those who undertake a program design project must be sensitive to this and be prepared to deal with it through appropriate strategies.[9]

(4) Routinization. A program change is no longer viewed as something new when it becomes part of the common services routinely provided. Routinization means that a technology or method is no longer on trial but is now accepted. Routinization is complete when a local agency can no longer return to a previous way of doing something, although some new proposal may appear to replace the routinized one. In this final stage, however, the program change is likely to look different, sometimes substantially different, from when it was first introduced.

According to Robert K. Yin, failure at the routinization stage can be more costly than failure during adoption or implementation.[10] This is because a program change is likely to have incurred full-scale costs and shown some benefits, unlike change that may have failed at the implementation stage. In addition, failure to routinize can be very costly for those persons who have been associated with a program change; they may have invested large amounts of time in developing skills associated with a program change, often at the expense of foregoing other opportunities. An important finding in Yin's research is that if routinization is to succeed, practitioners must see clear benefits to themselves either in terms of convenience, reduced physical effort, safety while on the job, or the elimination of distasteful tasks. In addition, top administrators must provide support. Yin elaborates as follows:

These top administrators are usually an essential part of the key decisions about an innovation—e.g., whether to adopt and try it in the first place, whether to make staff available through some ad hoc arrangements (e.g., overtime or special hours) or whether to make budgetary funds available each year. Without administrative support, most innovations will fail to become routinized . . . .[11]

THE PROGRAM DESIGN PROCESS

The task that lies ahead in the present work is to translate knowledge of change into methods of program design. This is to ask: given various public needs, how does one go about designing a program to best meet any of those needs? The underlying rationale is to be able to guide change from the perspective of the practitioner or decision maker who is striving to develop and improve public programs under real-time conditions.

To this end, we draw from the problem-solver and organizational change models reviewed in the previous section. The problem-solver model represents the normative-advisory approach to program change. As previously noted, this requires defining the problem, searching for solutions, selecting the 'best' solution, and applying it. A basic assumption here is that there is value in decision making that uses rational planning concerning the expected outcomes of various alternatives. Program change through rational planning, however, will not succeed if the organization cannot support it. It must be supplemented, therefore, by knowledge of organizational change.

The organizational change model views program change as necessarily moving through various stages from preadoption, to adoption, to implementation, to routinization. The change object may fail to be adopted or implemented or routinized, or may be significantly modified along the way, depending on various factors in the organizational setting that either facilitate it or impede it. As previously discussed, this includes such factors as the availability of professional staff, the advantages of a program change as perceived by agency personnel, and whether strong leadership can be counted on. Any attempt to design a program must account for as many of these factors as possible in the preadoption stage by anticipating how they are likely to affect the transfer of the change object at each subsequent stage and by devising appropriate strategies to deal with them.

Figure 1.2 illustrates the program design process as based on key aspects of the problem-solver and organizational change models. As shown here, program design is organized around ten basic work tasks which comprise a program design project. In each of the chapters that follow, these tasks are broken down into specific steps to further guide the reader. Not every task need be followed exactly as described in the text. The intent, rather, is to convey an agenda of basic considerations for those who are in the process of designing a program. For example, costs of time and money may preclude consulting all information sources for the purpose of generating and screening program alternatives as recommended in the text.

Chapter Two explains how to begin a program design project (task 1). This involves selecting a problem area for analysis and getting organized to do the project. Using the organizational change model, the basic interest in Chapter Three is how to identify organizational factors that can facilitate or impede program change (task 2). When an organization is

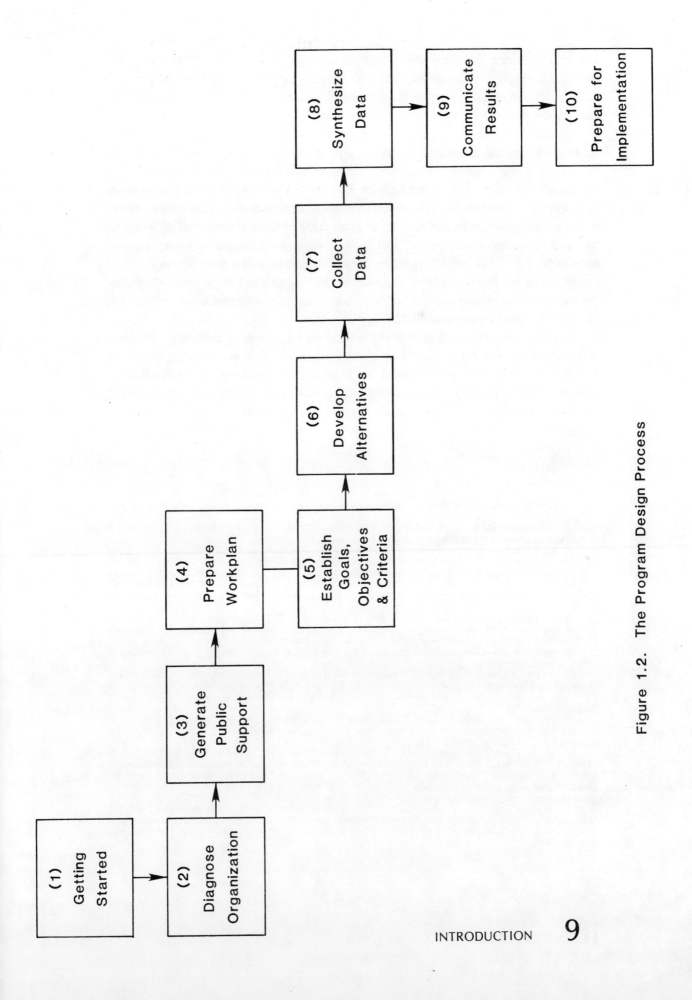

Figure 1.2. The Program Design Process

not likely to change, and when change strategies are not identified, then a program design project is not likely to be successful. Similarly Chapter Four deals with the need to generate public support in behalf of program change (task 3). This requires identifying key actors and determining strategies for overcoming political obstacles.

Chapter Five focuses on the preparation of a workplan which serves the purpose of showing what will be involved in conducting a program design project (task 4). The idea is that everyone with a stake in the project should know ahead of time what is to be done with few unexpected surprises to impede progress. Chapters Six to Nine are based essentially on rational problem-solving. These cover defining goals, objectives and performance criteria (task 5), developing alternatives (task 6), and collecting and synthesizing data on which to base a recommended solution (tasks 7 and 8). However, any recommendation is not likely to go very far if it is not properly packaged for decision makers who must act on it. Thus, Chapters Ten and Eleven deal with follow-up procedures such as how to write and review draft reports, how to communicate findings (task 9), and how to organize and monitor implementation to better assure routinization (task 10).

A related aspect, not covered in the present work, is program evaluation. Program evaluation measures the degree to which a program has actually achieved its intended goals and objectives *after* it has been adopted and implemented. While program evaluation has received a great deal of attention in the literature,[12] however, program design has received only scant attention.[13] It is to fill this unfortunate gap that the present monograph is dedicated.

NOTES

1. See Weiss, Carol H., *Evaluation Research* (Englewood Cliffs, NJ: Prentice Hall, Inc., 1972), pp. 4, 5.

2. See Zaltman, Gerald and Duncan, Robert, *Strategies for Planned Change* (New York: John Wiley & Sons, 1977), pp. 12, 13.

3. This is developed by Yin, Robert K., et al., *A Review of Case Studies of Technological Innovations in State and Local Services* (Santa Monica, CA: The Rand Corporation, February, 1976), pp. 4, 5.

4. See, for example, Bertcher, Harvey J., *Group Participation* (Beverly Hills: Sage Publications, 1979); Silverman, Phyllis R., *Mutual Help Groups* (Beverly Hills: Sage Publications, 1980).

5. See, for example, Yates, Douglas, *Neighborhood Democracy: The Politics and Impacts of Decentralization* (Lexington, MA: Lexington Books, D.C. Heath and Co., 1973); also, Yates, Douglas, and Yin, Robert K., *Street-Level Governments, Assessing Decentralization and Urban Services* (Lexington, MA: Lexington Books, 1975).

6. Dewey, John, *How We Think* (Boston: D.C. Heath & Co., 1910; 2nd edition, 1933).

7. Havelock, Ronald E., *Planning for Innovations Through Dissemination and Utilization of Knowledge* (Ann Arbor, MI: Center for Research on Utilization of Scientific Knowledge, 1969), p. 2–42.

8. See Lambright, W. Henry, *Technology Transfer to Cities: Processes of Choice at the Local Level* (Boulder, CO: Westview Press, 1979).

9. See Rein, Martin, and Rabinowitz, Francine, "Implementation: A Theoretical Perspective," in Burnham, Walter D., and Weinberg, Martha W., eds., *American Politics and Public Policy* (Cambridge, MA: M.I.T. Press, 1978); also Nakamura, Robert T., and Smallwood, Frank, *The Politics of Policy Implementation* (New York: St. Martin's Press, 1980).

10. Yin, Robert K., *Changing Urban Bureaucracies* (Lexington, MA: Lexington Books, 1979), p. 5.

11. ———, "Life Histories of Innovation: How Practices Become Routinized," *Public Administration Review*, Vol. 41 (January/February 1981), p. 27.

12. See, for example, Campbell, Donald T., "Reforms as Experiments," *American Psychologist*, Vol. 24 (April, 1969), pp. 409–429; Rossi, Peter H. and Freeman, Howard E., *Evaluation: A Systematic Approach* (Beverly Hills: Sage Publications, 2nd ed., 1982); Struening, Elmer L., and Guttentag, Marcia, *Handbook of Evaluation Research*, Vols. 1 and 2 (Beverly Hills: Sage Publications, 1975); Weiss, Carol H., *Evaluation Research: Methods of Assessing Program Effectiveness* (Englewood Cliffs, NJ: Prentice Hall, 1972).

13. See Hatry, Harry et al., *Program Analysis for State and Local Government* (Washington, DC: The Urban Institute, 1976); Public Technology, Inc., *Program Evaluation and Analysis* (Washington, DC: U.S. Department of Housing and Urban Development, Nov., 1978); Quade, E.S., *Analysis for Public Decisions* (New York: American Elsevier, 1975).

_____ CHAPTER 2

GETTING STARTED _____

The first task in undertaking a program design project is getting started. This means selecting a problem area for analysis and then organizing to do the project. This initial stage is probably more of a challenge to the person who does not work in a public or nonprofit agency and who sees himself/herself as something of an outsider to the public arena. Such a person must do a little more digging to find a topic and to organize around it, as compared to an "in-service" person who is aware through daily work activities of a number of issues that require attention and can more readily draw on the assistance of others.

STEP 1—SELECTING A PROBLEM AREA FOR ANALYSIS

Public problems are unrealized values, needs or opportunities which may be dealt with through public action. Problems may initially be discerned through the identification of symptoms. On any particular day, the daily newspaper provides information about such situations as rising unemployment, a crime wave, drunken driving, child abuse, deteriorating water quality, low test scores in the schools, detection of a new disease, etc. This represents one source for identifying a problem area for analysis.* Another strategy is to scrutinize your own agency for a problem area that is meaningful to you in your work. Different examples of problem areas are presented in Exhibit 2.1. Before a final choice is made, however, you should consult other sources and prepare a list of possible subjects. The best way to establish such a list is to examine the most common sources for suggestions as presented below.

_____
*To the extent that a problem lacks precise definition, we call it a problem area. Defining the problem is discussed in Chapter Five.

EXHIBIT 2.1. PROBLEM AREAS. The following are examples of different kinds of problem areas in which to do a program design project.

Public Safety

1. In order for law enforcement authorities to combat crime and maintain social order, there must be mutual understanding and cooperation between the police and local citizens. This, however, is difficult to achieve in black and Hispanic neighborhoods where citizen complaints of police abuse are considerably higher than in nonminority neighborhoods.

2. An analysis of vandalism in the schools shows that it has been increasing steadily over the past five years. This has been more pronounced on the east side of town, an area of middle class residents. School and law enforcement authorities have not been able to identify any strategies to effectively control such vandalism.

3. Cases of arson in the downtown business district have increased sharply during the past year. Bars and restaurants appear to be more vulnerable than other types of businesses.

Social Services

1. According to the most recent census figures, the number of retired elderly has increased by 20% over the past ten years. Social agency planners have noted the absence of educational programming for the elderly. They contend that senior citizens are a wasted resource. While most persons over sixty-five years are capable and mobile, their potential to fulfill useful jobs is not being realized because of the absence of educational opportunity.

2. As more and more cases of child abuse and neglect are reported, there is growing concern that social agencies have no clear or consistent guidelines for intervening in family situations where such behavior is known. This is all the more critical where there is a recurring pattern of abuse.

3. Approximately 3,000 single adults and 1,200 families (4,800 parents and children) inhabit city shelter and welfare hotels. Though many are discharged mental patients, they are also drug and alcohol addicts and unemployed persons who are presently receiving no counseling or rehabilitation assistance.

Health Services

1. Hospitals are operating at 75% of capacity although medical economists believe that 85% would be the optimum figure. This suggests a surplus of beds even as hospital costs continue to escalate.

2. Inspite of improvements in health-care delivery, the disparity between the quality of medical care available to the affluent and that available to the poor persists. There are few private practitioners in the poverty areas of the inner city. The poor also find that many physicians refuse to take Medicaid patients.

3. Delinquent youth evidence high levels of drinking problems. Over 38% of all inmates convicted and jailed for drunkenness, vagrancy or disorderly conduct charges are under twenty years of age.

Housing

1. Although some public housing projects have long waiting lists, others have high vacancy and turnover rates. This would seem to indicate differences in perception of safety and well-being among tenants in different projects.
2. The abandonment of low-cost private housing in certain inner-city neighborhoods has become increasingly prevalent. At the same time, there is a growing demand for low cost housing that can meet housing-code standards.

Transportation

1. Public transit ridership in rail and buses increased to a peak level in 1980. Since then it has been in decline. During nonrush hours and on weekends, transit is little used—an important factor in transit deficits.
2. The Public Transit Authority reports that the number of buses garaged for repairs has increased from an average of fifteen a month to thirty a month over the past two years.

Recreation

1. Attendance figures for neighborhood recreation centers show a decline during the fall and spring of each year over the past three years. This means less than optimal use of recreation staff and facilities.
2. Although attendance figures have been increasing, budget cutbacks for summer recreation programs mean that some programs may have to be dropped.

Solid Waste

1. About 75% of municipal waste is disposed of in open dumps and 13% in sanitary landfills. Citizens have been complaining about the aesthetics of such arrangements and the possible leaching of waste products into underground water sources.

1. Sources for Suggestions

Line agencies. Department heads and other agency personnel are usually aware of problems being addressed by programs. Sometimes problems are referred to in reports or budget requests for new programs or the revision of existing programs.

Staff agencies. Staff personnel working in the chief executive's office or in budget, planning or research usually have special insights into how government programs are or are not working with respect to specific community needs.

Elected officials. Mayors, councilmen, legislators and other elected officials are often aware of public problems as policy issues to be used in election campaigns or policy making.

Community organizations. Civic groups, neighborhood groups and special interest groups typically focus on issues pertinent to their needs.

Needs survey. Government jurisdictions are beginning to rely increasingly on sample surveys of citizens and other more specialized population clusters to identify particular needs and gaps in the provision of services.

Public records data. Census reports, law enforcement records, public health records, public assistance records, and education records are sources of information for identifying populations where the probable need for human services is great.

2. Screening the List

After the list of possible problems has been compiled, it should be screened to select the most appropriate one for analysis. This can be accomplished by using the following criteria.

Significance. How significant is the problem in terms of social, economic, or political impacts?

Performance. What program(s) addresses the problem and does there appear to be room for improving performance?

Community support. Is there evidence of interest and support from other persons and groups in the community to deal with the problem?

Information. To what extent is information available to help you better define the problem?

Capabilities. Are skills, time, money and other necessary resources available to carry out a program design project with respect to the problem?

To help you in the screening process, an interview guide is presented in Exhibit 2.2 which can be adapted to different problem areas. Where time permits, it can be used for canvassing various informed individuals in the community who are familiar with a range of problem areas. In this case, the problem area being assessed is alcohol abuse among teenagers.

STEP 2—ORGANIZING FOR PROGRAM DESIGN

Once a problem area is selected for program design, it is then necessary to establish the organizational means of carrying it out. A program design project can be undertaken by a single individual either on a full-time or part-time basis. In the present text, this person will be referred to as the 'analyst'. While a background in administration and research is desirable, it is more important that the analyst be inquisitive and resourceful. Any staff member, board member, volunteer, and even service consumer can initiate a project. Students should find it to be a good learning experience.

In doing a program design, the analyst should rely on the organizational change model. This means that the analyst must be able to induce broad involvement from others whose cooperation is necessary for the successful completion of the project. At some point, top management and sometimes policy makers should participate to better assure their support. Agency staff should also be consulted for necessary information, and specialists from other departments should be encouraged to contribute their expertise to supplement the more general skills of the analyst.

In light of this, a program design project should be viewed as a team effort requiring project management capabilities. This is to say, a project has its own organization, objectives and staffing needs. The team should consist of a group of people representing different skills and disciplines related to the program, brought together for the specific purpose of designing

EXHIBIT 2.2. INTERVIEW GUIDE: KEY INFORMANT CONTACT FORM. The following guide for interviewing key informants can be used to screen identified problem areas. This is illustrated in the area of alcohol abuse among teen-agers.

1. Of the problems that are seriously hurting the youth of this community, which five do you consider the most important?
   a.
   b.
   c.
   d.
   e.

2. Which one of the five you just mentioned do you consider is the most important?

3. If alcohol abuse is not mentioned, ask: In the general context of the problems among teen-agers, would you say alcohol abuse is a very important problem _____, somewhat important _____, not important at all _____?
   a. If important, what are some of the consequences (social, political, economic) for the community?

4. Why do you think so many young people are using alcohol?

5. Do you think the health and social service agencies in the community are doing an adequate job in working on the youth alcohol problem?
   a. What could they do better?

6. What would you be willing to contribute to an alcohol abuse program:
   a. _____ Particular skill _____ (Type)
   b. _____ Money _____ (Amount)
   c. _____ Time _____ (Specify)
   d. _____ Facilities
   e. _____ Data
   f. _____ Clerical help
   g. _____ Other _____

SOURCE: Adapted from the National Institute on Alcohol Abuse and Alcoholism, *Planning A Prevention Program*. Rockville, Maryland, April, 1977, pp. A-5, 6.

or redesigning the program. (Henceforth, the terms 'designing' and 'redesigning' will be used interchangeably.) The group may subsequently monitor at least the early phases of the program's implementation, and it should be terminated when its mission has been deemed accomplished.[1]

While it is likely that members of the team will be drawn from the problem area being analysed because of their expertise, an effort should be made to bring in people who can also contribute a different perspective to the problem on which the program design is based. Where all the team members are closely associated with a particular kind of problem, they may be too close to it to be able to identify and substantiate different approaches to its solution. It may also be necessary to augment service personnel with an outside consultant to assist in a specialized task, e.g., statistical analysis or cost-accounting.

Another consideration is that if the project requires broad community support, as is the case for many projects in social or human services, it may be advisable to establish a community-based task force to provide planning feedback to the project team. This could include representatives of racial, ethnic, religious and neighborhood organizations that have some stake in the process as well as business groups and the media—i.e., radio, television, newspapers. Such a task force could help to reduce the chance of community alienation and prevent the possibility of misreading political and social power structures in the community. The selection of a task force, however, should wait until the community setting has been diagnosed as described in Chapter Four.

To provide overall direction, a team leader should be designated. This person is responsible for delegating tasks to team members and managing external political relations. In working with a smaller agency, the team leader could also perform a liaison role with other agencies in addition to performing the duties of an analyst. In working with a larger agency, these jobs may be parceled out among different individuals. Where the scope and time frame of the project are not overly extensive, the analyst is the only person who may be involved full-time on the project.

The team leader should also be seen as a change agent who guides the proposed program through the organization. Unless the team leader understands the organization change process, however, the program design project is not likely to succeed. The more that the team leader can create a need and a commitment to change while avoiding obstacles, the more successful the change attempt is likely to be. Focusing on change strategies discussed in Chapter Three, the team leader should be prepared to suggest different methods at appropriate stages that could help maintain a supportive agency environment.

SUMMARY

This chapter has emphasized the importance of preparing for program design before actually doing it. This requires selecting a problem area for analysis and developing the organizational means of carrying it out. A necessary strategy is to involve other persons whose interests and participation are necessary for the successful completion of the project. When they are willing, such persons can be members of the project team helping to implement the project, or they can be members of a community task force helping to provide feedback. In this way, a program design project has its own organization and staff. Stressing organizational change, a primary role of the team leader is to guide the proposed program through the organizational system by steering it through obstacles and generating support.

NOTES

1. For an overview of project management, see Cleland, David I., and King, William R., *Systems Analysis and Project Management,* 3rd ed. (New York: McGraw-Hill, 1983).

CHAPTER **3**

DIAGNOSING THE ORGANIZATIONAL SETTING ____

The degree to which program change is successfully achieved depends on the influence of various factors in the agency and its environment. After a problem area has been identified and the project team has been organized, the next step is for the team to diagnose the agency (or agencies) that has jurisdiction to identify the most critical factors in the organizational setting. Knowledge of such factors can help the team anticipate opportunities and impediments in the course of carrying out the program design project.

Five basic steps are involved in diagnosing an agency that has been targeted for change. They are: (1) describing the performance gap; (2) rating individual factors; (3) rating organizational factors; (4) rating environmental factors; and (5) assessing the feasibility of a program design project. Not all factors are important in each change situation. The listings presented below provide a guide, however, for the analyst to follow as he or she examines the setting.

STEP 1—DESCRIBING THE PERFORMANCE GAP

Stimulus for change in an organization occurs when there is a perceived discrepancy between how it is performing and how the organization or someone else believes it ought to be performing. This discrepancy is called a performance gap. In such situations, the organization feels that it ought to be doing better in its performance than it actually is. This, in turn, serves to provoke a search for alternative ways of performing.[1]

A performance gap can either be externally or internally induced. Referring to the former, for example, there can be a change in the service environment such as a new clientele to service, or a change in requirements, such as a mandate to reduce agency expenditures. Sometimes public perceptions of needs change as illustrated by increasing attention in recent years to the needs of the elderly and the handicapped. Furthermore, clients and citizen groups are becoming increasingly aggressive in pressing demands for improved services. On the other hand, there can also be a lessening of demand for an agency's services that instigates a search for alternative services.[2]

Viewing the internal aspects of an organization, a performance gap can be caused by the introduction of new personnel with different expectations of agency performance. Technological change, such as the introduction of a management information system, will tend to raise managers' expectations of what the new system can do for them. In addition, more and more agencies have been using program evaluations to determine how well they are performing. This often serves to stimulate a reexamination of existing operations where it is found that the agency is not realizing its program goals.

In doing program design, it is the responsibility of the analyst to determine the nature of the performance gap in the problem area selected for analysis. Such information is necessary for mapping out new service directions. When an existing program has been evaluated, this can be the source of very useful data for defining the performance gap. Otherwise, the analyst should interview appropriate agency administrators. The interview guide in Exhibit 3.1 is intended to assist this process as illustrated in the area of alcohol abuse among youth. Particularly important, here, is whether administrators recognize a performance gap. If they do not, it is not likely that they will cooperate in the program design project. Sometimes the interview process can serve to stimulate recognition of needs that require improved services. Responses to the questions should show whether services are perceived as being adequate and where there are community or client needs that are not being met.

EXHIBIT 3.1. INTERVIEW GUIDE: AGENCY CONTACT FORM. The following guide for interviewing agency administrators can be used to determine a performance gap(s) with respect to servicing a problem area. This is illustrated in the area of alcohol abuse among youth.

1. Agency name and location
   Name _____
   Street _____
   City _____
   Phone _____
   Contact person _____
   Date contacted _____

2. In the general context of problems among teen-agers, would you say alcohol abuse is a very important problem _____, somewhat important _____, not important at all _____?

---

3. What population do you work with?)
   a. General population   e. Male youth population
   b. Adult (18 and over)   f. Female youth population
   c. Teenagers (12-18)   g. Other _____
   d. Under 12

4. What services do you supply to the community?

5. Are you interested in collaborating on a youth alcohol abuse program in the
   community? Yes _____ No _____

6. What possible prevention strategies would you advocate?

   a. _____ Educational programs   d. _____ Job placement or training
   b. _____ Recreational programs   e. Other _____
   c. _____ Peer counseling

7. What resources would you be willing to supply in such an effort?
   a. _____ Information on cases or clients   f. _____ Transportation
   b. _____ Training for staff   g. _____ Money
   c. _____ Professional support services   h. _____ Equipment
              for clients   i. _____ Supplies
   d. _____ Volunteers   j. _____ Office Space
   e. _____ Administrative or clerical help   k. _____ Other

8. Can you suggest other sources of data (such as surveys or reports) or services
   (other agencies and programs)?

   Alcohol Service Agencies Only (9 to 12)
9. Do you provide any of these services? (Check all that apply)
   _____ Informational
           Number of clients per year _____   Ages _____
   _____ Educational programs
           Number of clients per year _____   Ages _____
   _____ Prevention programs
           Number of clients per year _____   Ages _____
   _____ Outreach programs
           Number of clients per year _____   Ages _____
   _____ Treatment, residential
           Number of clients per year _____   Ages _____
   _____ Detoxification
           Number of clients per year _____   Ages _____

10. Of the services listed above, which ones require development or expansion in
    order to better meet community or client needs?

11. What is the estimation of the age, sex, ethnic group and societal features of your
    client population?
    a. Ages: _____ through _____
    b. Sex: Males _____ Females _____
    c. Ethnic: White _____% Black _____% Other _____%
    d. Income: Low _____% Average _____% High _____%

e. What form of alcohol does the typical client use?
   Beer _____ Wine _____ Liquor _____ Combination _____
f. Frequency of use:
   _____ One drink or less per month
   _____ One per week
   _____ 2-3 per day
   _____ 4-5 per day

12. What client groupings (age, sex, ethnicity, etc.) do you estimate require more or improved servicing? Explain why.

SOURCE: National Institute on Alcohol Abuse and Alcoholism, *Planning A Prevention Program.* Rockville, Maryland, April 1977, pp. A-7 to A-10.

The perceptions of the producers of a service, however, may differ from those who receive the service. To test for this, it is recommended that a random sample of clients also be interviewed using the interview guide in Exhibit 3.2. Where time and resources are limited, the analyst and project team will have to decide how to minimize their efforts in gathering information.[3]

EXHIBIT 3.2. INTERVIEW GUIDE: CLIENT RESPONSE FORM. These questions are meant to be a general guide to be adapted to specific situations. Questioning should be preceded by a brief explanation of the purpose of the interview.

1. What do you think about drinking?
   (If he/she talks about youth who drink too much, ask:)
   a. Why do you think some young people drink too much?
   b. How do you think the problem could be alleviated?

2. What about alcohol and drugs? Is there any concern you have that would require a combined approach? Please explain.

3. In what prevention activities or alcohol education programs have you participated?
   a. Where did the activity occur?
   b. When?
   c. Who sponsored it?

4. What was your role in that activity (e.g., planner, advisor, participant)?

5. What did you particularly like about the activity?

6. What did you particularly dislike?

7. How would you have done it differently had it been up to you?
   (Answer this question in terms of content and delivery.)

SOURCE: National Institute on Alcohol Abuse and Alcoholism, *Planning A Prevention Program.* Rockville. Maryland, April 1977, p. A-12.

Exercise 3.1

As outlined in Exercise 3.1, the reader should now examine the problem area that he or she has selected for analysis and specify as precisely as possible what is the need(s) or problem in the community or among clients that requires attention. Use hard data wherever possible as indicators of the need(s)—for example, reported new cases of child abuse, number of reported crimes per 1000 population, or the percentage of unemployed. The location, time span, and the rate of increase or decrease should also be specified (e.g., from 121 per thousand to 150 per thousand) where such information is available. Following this, you should then determine the extent to which the need(s) is being provided for through existing services. In doing this, use information that has been generated from interviews as well as whatever documentary sources that may be available. Where certain needs are not being met, describe the deficiency by referring to types of groups being excluded from services or clients who report unmet needs. Finally, list types of services that should be added if not presently available, or that should be developed in order to close the performance gap.

EXERCISE 3.1. DESCRIBING THE PERFORMANCE GAP

1. Viewing the problem area that you have selected for analysis, what is the need(s) being addressed? What are indicators of this need(s)? (For example, reported new cases of child abuse; percentage of unemployed.) Where possible, specify location, time span, and rate of increase or decrease.

2. Is the identified need(s) being adequately provided for through existing services?

                              _____ Yes   _____No

If not, describe the deficiency. (For example, certain groups that are consistently left out or clients who report unmet needs.)

3. To better meet the identified need(s), what services should be added or developed?

STEP 2—RATING INDIVIDUAL FACTORS

—Attitudes of key decision makers
—Aversion to risk
—Maximizing rewards
—Job satisfaction

Studies show that when a performance gap is defined, the attitudes of key decision makers are crucial in determining a remedy. As a rule, these are persons who control organization sanctions such as salaries and working conditions. They serve as a central link between demands and ideas from the outside and program change within the organization. Particularly significant is the degree to which their ideological bent is either in support of change or against change. Where a status quo ideology prevails or where a performance gap is not recognized, program change is not likely to occur or will at least be slowed.[4]

Viewing all personnel within the organization, an individual's aversion to risk is another important consideration. The more unwilling administrators are to take risks, the less likely are they to gamble on change where political and economic stakes are involved. For example, employee unions are usually concerned about the threat to jobs and status posed by new technologies and will tend to oppose them unless proper assurances can be given. This is in contrast to more open or 'modern' orientations where change is promoted as a rational approach to dealing with problems. Academics, trained professional administrators, and consultants, who are more inclined to take a long-run view, usually reflect such values.

Underlying such behavior is personal desire for aggrandizement. This can cause inertia where the benefits of maintaining the status quo are greater than the costs; or, it can instigate change where the rewards for change are greater than the costs. "The greatest of such rewards are gains in power, income and prestige associated with increases in the resources controlled by a given official or a given bureau."[5] In light of this, negotiations between competing parties on any issue should explore various tradeoffs which assure all parties that they can maximize their gains from a particular outcome.

If organizations are to accommodate change, moreover, they must maintain morale and loyalty among employees. Morale and loyalty tend to decline where job satisfaction declines. Persons who are satisfied with their jobs are more committed to the organization and are, therefore, more receptive to proposals for improving existing methods. If people are very dissatisfied, they may simply withdraw from the situation and make no effort to change.[6]

Exercise 3.2

At this point, the reader is asked to pause and consider how individual factors that have just been discussed are likely to influence program change in the agency being diagnosed. As based on information generated through observation and/or interviews, score each factor listed in Exercise 3.2 to the best of your ability. Where key decision makers do not agree as to the existence of a performance gap, and where agency personnel are risk-averse and see few benefits for themselves, it is not likely that the agency will be amenable to a program change.

In such instances, you may wish to consider strategies to create a more amenable climate. For example, provide reading material or bring in a consultant as the source of new information to key decision makers; or institute a capacity-building workshop for staff. (See Table 3.1).

EXERCISE 3.2. RATING INDIVIDUAL FACTORS. Viewing the target agency, score each of the following individual factors on a scale from high to low.

1. To what extent do key decision makers recognize a performance gap?

High _____ Low
　　　4　　　　3　　　　2　　　　1　　　　0

2. Are key decision makers likely to be supportive of program change?

High _____ Low
　　　4　　　　3　　　　2　　　　1　　　　0

3. To what extent are agency personnel inclined to take risks for program change?

High _____ Low
　　　4　　　　3　　　　2　　　　1　　　　0

4. To what extent are agency personnel likely to see benefits in program change?

High _____ Low
　　　4　　　　3　　　　2　　　　1　　　　0

5. To what extent is agency morale likely to be supportive of program change?

High _____ Low
　　　4　　　　3　　　　2　　　　1　　　　0

6. Other factors (specify).

High _____ Low
　　　4　　　　3　　　　2　　　　1　　　　0

STEP 3—RATING ORGANIZATIONAL FACTORS

—Slack resources
—Complexity
—Centralization-decentralization
—Formalization
—Information flow

An important organizational factor which influences program change is the availability of slack resources. Richard Cyert and James March define slack as the difference between payments required to maintain the organization and the resources obtained from the environment.[7] Access to extra funds encourages change, especially in large and successful organizations. Where resources are constrained, new products or methods with a high initial cost are likely to be rejected.

Other considerations refer primarily to the degree of complexity, centralization and formalization that is evident in organizations. Complexity is based on the degree of specialization in an organization. The presence of many specialists representing different fields is likely to increase the quality and variety of information flowing into an organization. This, in turn, contributes to a greater awareness of performance problems as well as possible solutions for dealing with them.[8] Furthermore, the more diverse the occupational and professional mix of personnel, the greater the source of organizational conflict which leads, in turn, to a greater number of proposals for change.

Centralization refers to the locus of authority and decision making in the organization. "The greater the hierarchy of authority and the less participation that exists in the organization, the greater the centralization" and vice versa.[9] The effects of centralization on change are somewhat fuzzy. Where information flows vertically through the hierarchy with only limited opportunity for communication and interaction across functional divisions, performance gaps are not as easily discerned and solutions which emanate from the outlying perimeters are constrained. Ronald G. Havelock explains that centralization increases the number of gatekeepers through which proposals for change must pass.[10] The inertia of some of the largest centralized public welfare and mental health systems serve as useful illustrations.

Nor are the benefits of decentralization clear. Havelock notes that decentralization can serve as a barrier to change where affected units are able to exercise veto power over solutions proposed at some central superior level.[11] Jerald Hage and Michael Aiken see it differently. They claim that decentralization promotes conflict among units that facilitates the introduction of new programs.[12] These different points of view may be attributed to the fact that the scholars fail to make a clear distinction between the initiation of change and the implementation of change. This is to say that centralization may not be supportive of proposals for change, but may be supportive of implementation.

According to James Q. Wilson, the climate required to induce the adoption of change in organizations may be the same climate that will prohibit the implementation of change.[13] Large, open organizations that invite different points of view are more likely to promote new ideas; but those ideas may never be implemented if a consensus and a pulling together doesn't take place after the idea has been adopted.

Another factor to be considered is the degree of organizational formalization. This pertains to the emphasis placed on following specific rules and procedures. What studies we have on the subject suggest that the greater the formalization, the less likely it is that an organization will be able to accommodate change: there is always some rule that gets in the way. Highly formalized public bureaucracies are especially resistant to innovation and change.[14]

In viewing the internal functioning of an organization, the flow of information through the system is another important factor. Where breakdowns in communication are likely, and where certain groups in the administrative hierarchy fail to receive information, decisions for program change are not very feasible.

Exercise 3.3

As presented in Exercise 3.3, the reader should now examine various organizational factors and rate them as to the extent to which they are likely to support program change. Per-

EXERCISE 3.3. RATING ORGANIZATIONAL FACTORS. Viewing the target agency, rate each of the following factors on a scale from high to low.

1. To what extent are extra funds and other resources available for the support of program change?

High _____ Low
    4   3   2   1   0

2. To what extent does there appear to be a good mix of occupational and professional personnel for the support of program change? Are they cooperative?

High _____ Low
    4   3   2   1   0

3. To what extent does there appear to be open participation and communication for the support of program change?

High _____ Low
    4   3   2   1   0

4. To what extent does there appear to be sufficient flexibility in rules and procedures to accommodate program change?

High _____ Low
    4   3   2   1   0

5. To what extent are information sources available for the support of program change?

High _____ Low
    4   3   2   1   0

6. Other factors (specify).

High _____ Low
    4   3   2   1   0

sons who have no direct experience with the target agency will have to rely primarily on interviews of agency administrators and other informants. Some questions that could be asked are: To your knowledge, are there any specific rules or procedures that are likely to prevent or make it difficult to achieve a program change? How many others in the agency are expected to participate in decisions related to the program change? Other members of the project team who are associated with the target agency can be especially helpful in generating information here.

STEP 4—IDENTIFYING ENVIRONMENTAL FACTORS

—Market-related factors
—Citizens or clients
—Community leaders
—Other organizations
—Government agencies

To better comprehend the potential for change, it is necessary to account for the environment in which an organization functions. This is because organizations receive various inputs from their environment, process them, and feed back finished products. Where inputs become strong enough, otherwise reluctant organizations may become open to change. Most notable are market-related factors such as sudden changes in technology or crises which affect demand for an agency's services. In such situations, an organization must be able to change its methods, particularly where demand for a service declines. Viewing the economic environment, the frequency of change is likely to increase when the market for a service is expanding. Also, when the cost of a particular input rises or when funding is reduced, an agency will usually attempt to eliminate the use of that element in producing the service.

The market for public services is somewhat more complex than it is for private services. This is because citizen influence on the product is not as direct as is the case for the consumer of private services. Donald Menzel, for example, states that administrators in many service areas regard the public as being unable to evaluate the quality of agency performance except, perhaps, by noting highly visible features such as new equipment, e.g., garbage trucks.[15] The difficulty in evaluating the activities of public service agencies is that it is nearly impossible for clients to judge whether or not an agency is using the best practices and techniques.

It should not be concluded, however, that citizen influence on public agencies is totally absent. Direct citizen or client action tends to work more like a veto than a stimulant. Menzel explains that the effect of anticipated citizen reactions usually works more effectively where there is a direct relationship between the agency and the public it serves. Garbage collection, for example, is regarded as an area that is highly resistant to reform. Despite a plethora of studies that show once-a-week curbside pick-ups save tax dollars, city officials in many communities are reluctant to change the system for fear of antagonizing citizens.

In addition to citizens and clients who receive the service, it is important to assess the kind of support likely to be forthcoming from various community leaders, officials, and organizations that have a stake in the agency or the problem area. This should also include the mass media (TV, newspapers) whose support is often critical. The role of other government jurisdictions must also be taken into account. Especially influential are various federal and state government requirements that are mandated through grant programs and that have served to stimulate local agencies to adopt new ways of doing things.

Federal grant programs can be counterproductive, however, when localities adopt programs primarily because of the availability of funds. Because such programs are often terminated when federal funds run out, the federal government has been striving to shift responsibility for most social programs to the state and local levels.[16] The assumption is that where programs are generated and funded by the same agency or jurisdiction that is to administer them, they will have a higher probability of successful implementation.

Exercise 3.4

Relying on observations, interviews, and available documentation, the reader should now assess how various environmental factors are likely to influence program change. The ratings provide an opportunity to identify sources of opposition before the program design gets underway. This assessment could also be used to identify particular community actors and groups that could comprise a supporting coalition. This information should be considered subsequently during the program design stage on the question of how to mollify key groups. If the opposition forces can be reduced or removed through certain modifications in the program proposal while the supportive forces are retained or enhanced, it is likely that program change can be achieved. (Methods of generating public support are presented in Chapter Four.)

EXERCISE 3.4. RATING ENVIRONMENTAL FACTORS. Viewing the environment of the target agency, to what extent are each of the following factors likely to support program change?

1. Market-related factors

High _____ Low
     4   3   2   1   0

2. Citizens or clients who receive the service

High _____ Low
     4   3   2   1   0

3. Other organizations as interest groups

High _____ Low
     4   3   2   1   0

4. The mass media (TV, newspapers)

High _____ Low
     4   3   2   1   0

5. Other government agencies (federal, state, local)

High _____ Low
     4   3   2   1   0

6. Other factors (specify).

High _____ Low
     4   3   2   1   0

STEP 5—ASSESSING THE FEASIBILITY OF A PROGRAM DESIGN PROJECT

The reader should now select a program design project as based on his or her diagnosis of the target agency (or agencies). It is important in this early stage that the 'right' choice be made. This means that a need or problem has been shown to exist and that decision makers acknowledge a performance gap. Where this is not the case, and where resistance is detected, another problem area may have to be considered for analysis; or, where enough time is available, change strategies listed in Table 3.1 could be utilized to help make the organizational climate more open to change.

Other criteria in assessing the feasibility of a program design project are:

—the availability of information sources to support analysis;

—the availability of resources in personnel, funds, and skills to do the project;

—the extent to which there are political obstacles, e.g., other agencies or interest groups that may be opposed;

—the extent to which there are organizational obstacles, e.g., a highly centralized administrative structure or too many formal rules;

—the availability of time to complete the project before a formal decision is to be made about the program change.

After weighing these criteria, the reader should prepare a project selection paper by responding to questions listed in Exhibit 3.3. This should not be difficult where the diagnosis of the target agency has been successfully completed. The project selection paper could also include suggested organizational strategies to promote a climate for change. The paper should be no longer than two or three typewritten pages in order to facilitate review by program personnel and other likely participants. Such review in the early stages can be done through informal discussion and is useful for setting a cooperative tone among decision makers and practitioners.

SUMMARY

This chapter has relied on the organizational change model for diagnosing the agency setting prior to undertaking a program design project. Program change cannot be imposed as if in a void. The completed exercises are intended to assist the analyst in selecting the most

TABLE 3.1. STRATEGIES FOR ORGANIZATIONAL CLIMATES CONDUCIVE TO CHANGE.

Individuals in Organizations	Organizational Structure
Allow greater participation in decision making.	Decentralization and alternating temporary structures.
Participation in special project teams and quality circles.	
Encourage information exchange.	Improve communication channels.
Encourage suggestions.	
Participation in R&D and planning groups involving different ranks and functional specialists.	
Each person should spend at least 50% of time on one project.	Functional specialization.
Participation in special skill training.	
Participation in team projects and intergroup activities.	Organizational development and functional interdependence.
Participation in team-building workshops.	
Utilization of process consultation activities.	
Encourage proficiency in data gathering and organizational diagnosis.	Evaluation and research.
Reliance on survey feedback activities.	

EXHIBIT 3.3. PROJECT SELECTION PAPER. Below is an outline for gauging the feasibility of a program design project. The completed paper should be no longer than two or three typewritten pages.

1. What is the problem(s) or need(s) addressed by the current program?

2. What evidence is there of a performance gap(s)?

3. Elaborate on whether a new program should be designed with new goals and objectives to deal with the problem(s) or need(s) or whether the present program should be redesigned with new alternatives to meet existing goals and objectives.

4. Other considerations:
   a. How difficult is information collection?
   b. Are there sufficient resources in terms of personnel, funds, and skills to do the project?
   c. How supportive are management and personnel?
   d. What are the political obstacles?
   e. What are the organizational obstacles?
   f. What are the time constraints?

5. What special promotional strategies could be used to establish a climate for change? (This question should be answered only where such tactics appear to be necessary.)

appropriate program design given various organizational conditions. These covered an assessment of the performance gap and ratings of individual factors, organizational factors and environmental factors. Where necessary, change strategies could be used to make the organizational climate more conducive to change. The project selection paper which helps to assess the feasibility of designing a particular program represents the end product of this initial stage.

NOTES

1. Downs, Anthony, *Inside Bureaucracy* (Boston: Little Brown & Company, 1966) p.169.

2. See Zaltman and Duncan, *Strategies*, pp. 24–26.

3. See Neuber, Keith *et al.*, *Needs Assessment, A Model for Community Planning* (Beverly Hills: Sage Publications, 1980).

4. Baldridge, J. Victor and Burnham, Robert A., "Organizational Innovation: Individual, Organizational and Environmental Impacts," *Administrative Science Quarterly*, June 1975, Vol. 20, No. 2, p. 169.

5. Downs, *Inside Bureaucracy*, p. 2.

6. Hage, Jerald and Aiken, Michael, "Program Change and Organization Properties: A Comparative Analysis," *The American Journal of Sociology*, Vol. 72, No. 5, March 1967, pp. 503–519.

7. Cyert, Richard and March, James, *A Behavioral Theory of the Firm* (New Jersey: Prentice-Hall, Inc., 1963), p. 36.

8. See Zaltman, Gerald, Duncan, Robert and Holbeck, Jonny, *Innovations and Organizations* (New York: John Wiley and Sons, Inc., 1973).

9. Zaltman and Duncan, *Strategies*, p. 265.

10. Havelock, *Planning for Innovations*, p. 6–24.

11. Havelock, *Planning for Innovations*, pp. 6–35, 36.

12. Hage and Aiken, *The American Journal of Sociology*.

13. Wilson, James Q., "Innovation in Organization: Notes Toward a Theory," in *Approaches to Organizational Design*, James D. Thompson, ed., (Pittsburgh: University of Pittsburgh Press, 1966) p. 200.

14. See Thompson, Victor A., "Bureaucracy and Innovation," *Administrative Science Quarterly*, Vol. 10, No. 1, June 1965, pp. 1–20.

15. Menzel, Donald, "Scientific and Technological Dimensions of Innovations in American States." Paper presented at the 1975 Annual Meeting of the Midwest Political Science Association, May 1-3, 1975, Chicago, Illinois.

16. See, for example, Berman, Paul and McLaughlin, Milbrey W., *Federal Programs Supporting Educational Change*, Vol. VIII, R-158918-HEW (Santa Monica, CA: Rand, 1978).

CHAPTER 4

GENERATING PUBLIC SUPPORT _____

In addition to diagnosing the organizational setting as discussed in the previous chapter, it is also necessary to examine the community setting as a basis for developing strategies which could induce public support for program change. Accordingly, the project team should identify relevant bureaucratic and political actors and attempt to determine what impact they are likely to have on the program. (This builds on the ratings in Exercise 3.4.) This should be done prior to the actual formulation of the program, for it is to the team's advantage to know in advance what political obstacles may be involved and to determine methods of overcoming them prior to the design of the program.

The process of estimating the impacts of various actors and defining support strategies as discussed in this chapter is based on the PRINCE Political Accounting System developed by William D. Coplin and Michael K. O'Leary.[1] Five steps are involved: (1) restating the problem as an issue; (2) identifying the likely actors; (3) estimating the issue position, power and salience for each actor; (4) calculating the weights and probabilities for each actor and for the whole system; and (5) identifying strategies for overcoming obstacles. Of course, where support or opposition to a program change is clearly overwhelming, the need to generate public support would not be necessary. Experience shows, however, that this is not usually the case.

STEP 1— RESTATING THE PROBLEM AS AN ISSUE

An issue is a pending decision or a course of action that is likely to generate controversy.

Having identified a problem for analysis, the project team must also attempt to clarify sources of disagreement about the problem and whether there will be sufficient support to remedy it. Certain groups that have a stake in the problem area may not agree that the problem is worth dealing with through program change. For example, some actors may not support the idea that air pollution is a serious problem to be addressed through public programs. They may argue that damage to the environment is a necessary price to pay for a capitalist economy. Another example is the contention that low reading scores of children in inner-city schools is a reflection of the inferior capabilities of low-income families and any attempt to deal with this through special programs would be to no avail.

At this stage, the analyst and project team should reformulate the problem statement (as presented in the project selection paper) into an issue statement. An issue statement serves to instigate agreement or disagreement as a way of discerning the likely alignment of various interests either in favor of change or against it. The key to phrasing an issue statement is to specify a verb at the beginning of the statement which indicates a required action. Some examples of verbs that can be used are 'permit', 'support', 'provide', or 'restrict'. Illustrations of issue statements as derived from problem statements in Exhibit 2.1 are presented in Exhibit 4.1. Needless to say, some statements will generate more controversy than others; but all will produce at least some differences of opinion among different interests.

EXHIBIT 4.1. ISSUE STATEMENTS. The following are examples of different issue statements derived from problem statements in Exhibit 2.1.

1. Provide educational opportunity for elderly persons over 65 years of age to enhance their potential for employment.
2. Provide activities to improve relations and cooperation between the police and low-income residents.
3. Restrict the number of hospital beds being made available in the community.
4. Reduce the number of public housing units in the community.
5. Provide remedial treatment to delinquent youths charged with drunkenness and/or disorderly conduct.
6. Establish clear guidelines for social agencies intervening in family situations involving child abuse.
7. Close all open dumps that are used for the disposal of solid waste.

STEP 2—IDENTIFYING THE LIKELY ACTORS

An actor is any individual, group, or organization that ought to be accounted for in designing a program or in implementing it after it has been adopted. Some programs can be developed and implemented with a minimal involvement of other actors, while other programs require the extensive involvement of many actors.

At least seven types of bureaucratic and political actors should be considered: (1) the overhead agencies, e.g., budget, personnel, purchasing, law; (2) other line agencies; (3) elected officials in the same government; (4) higher levels of government; (5) private-sector providers;

(6) special interest and community groups; and (7) the media. Each of these can affect a program in one or more of the following ways: by producing political support for, or attacks on, the proposed adoption of the program; by providing or withholding necessary authorizations and clearances; and by participating positively or negatively in the actual operations and management of the program.

In grouping the actors into categories, the following criteria should be applied.

1. Actors that have the same economic interests should be grouped together. In dealing with a housing issue for example, all building owners should be grouped in one category and all tenants should be grouped in another category.

2. Actors that have veto power should not be grouped together.

3. Actors should not be grouped together where there is disagreement among them or if they have widely unequal power. For example, a city government could be considered a single actor if there was agreement among all the members of the government on the issue and if each component had approximately equal power. On the other hand if disagreements were evident and if some components were more influential than others, distinctions should be made among separate actors.

4. Select a combination of actors that represent a reasonable picture of the overall system that surrounds the issue. Do not include an excess of actors that might give one side unrealistic weighting.

Viewing these guidelines, it should be recognized that the identification of actors is as much of an art as a science. Indeed, the judgement and insights of the analyst and project team are a critical element in the entire analysis. Coplin and O'Leary explain that this should not be viewed as a weakness since judgement is required in almost all forms of analysis.[2] Under the procedures outlined here, the intent is to organize and guide judgement as systematically as possible.

STEP 3—ESTIMATING THE ISSUE POSITION, POWER AND SALIENCE FOR EACH ACTOR

Once the key actors have been determined, they should be listed in the appropriate places in Exercise 4.1. The project team should then attempt to estimate the issue position, power and salience for each of the actors. Scoring procedures are described below. The more that the members of the team are familiar with the issue, the easier it will be to assign values in each category. Where disagreements occur, they should be resolved through discussion. If necessary, other knowledgeable individuals should be consulted.

Issue position is the present attitude of the actor toward the issue. It is scored on a scale from $+3$, $+2$, $+1$, depending on the degree of support, to -1, -2, -3, depending on the degree of opposition. On either extreme, a score of $+3$ represents strong support and a score of -3 represents strong opposition. A score of 0 indicates a neutral position. In estimating the issue position, team members should find out what the actor says about the issue either through a direct interview or through newspapers and other available sources. The team should also take stock of the actor's social, economic and political background and what its position is likely to be on the basis of self-interest. Where there is doubt, the team should weigh self-interest over verbal statements in assigning values.

EXERCISE 4.1. CONDUCTING AN ISSUE ANALYSIS

ISSUE:_____
(State in terms of a desired outcome using a phrase beginning with a verb.)

Actors	Issue Position	X	Power	X	Salience	=	Total Support by Actor
	−3—0—+3		1—3		1—3		
		X		X		=	
		X		X		=	
		X		X		=	
		X		X		=	
		X		X		=	
		X		X		=	
		X		X		=	
		X		X		=	

Totals: A—Scores of all actors supporting the issue: ____
         B— Absolute value of actors opposing the issue: _____
         C— Scores of actors with zero issue positions: _____
         D—Totals A, B, C: _____
         E— Total A + ½ of Total C: _____
         Probability of Support = $\dfrac{E}{D}$ = _____

SOURCE: The Prince System is explained in William D. Coplin and Michael K. O'Leary, *PS 23: Political Analysis Through the Prince System* (Croton-on-Hudson: Policy Studies Associates, 1983).

Power is the degree to which an actor can use influence to support or oppose an issue. Power is based on the kinds of resources that an actor can command such as money, social status, jobs, group following, institutional authority, knowledge or prestige. The more resources that are available to an individual or an organization, the more powerful such entities are likely to be. In estimating power, the project team should assign a 3 where it is determined that an actor has substantial power—especially if the actor can veto or prevent the implementation of a program. An actor should be assigned a 1 where power is minimal, and a 2 where it is moderate.

Salience refers to the degree of importance that an actor attaches to an issue. A score of 3, represents high salience, a score of 2 represents moderate salience, and a score of 1 represents low salience. When estimating salience, the team should deduce from the actor's social, political and economic background how much importance it attaches to an issue. The team should also attempt to determine the frequency and intensity with which the actor makes public statements about the issue. A note of caution, however, is that salience can be rapidly altered by changing events which impact an issue.

STEP 4—CALCULATING WEIGHTS AND PROBABILITIES

Exhibit 4.2 illustrates how to calculate weights for each actor and the overall probability of support for an issue. In this case the issue is whether to restrict the number of hospital beds in the community. The issue position of each actor may be scored either a negative or a positive depending on whether the actor supports the issue statement or is against it. A zero means the actor has no position on the issue. Power and salience are always positive. Multiplying the three factors gives either a negative weight or a positive weight.

Calculating the weights for each actor provides a profile view of how different groups are likely to influence the issue and helps the team identify which groups to target on. For example, if it is the case that the program will focus on options to restrict the number of hospital beds as a way of keeping costs down, then the hospital administrators, hospital staff and/or the physicians association would have to be persuaded to change their issue positions; and possibly the Community Health Board could be coaxed from a neutral position to a positive position. As can be seen a neutral score is put in parenthesis.

After the weights for each of the actors have been calculated, the analyst and project team should then estimate the overall probability of achieving program change. This is done as follows:

1. Add the scores of all the supporters. This total should be labeled A.
2. Add the scores of all those actors opposing the issue. This total should be labeled B.
3. Multiply the nonzero scores of all the actors that have a neutral issue position and then add them. This total should be labeled C.
4. Add the total for A and one-half of the total for C to estimate the total weight for the neutral actors. This should be labeled E. The reason the total for C is divided by half is the probability that neutral actors may be either supporters or opponents of the issue. The best way to deal with this situation is to include half of the neutral actors' scores

EXHIBIT 4.2. ISSUE ANALYSIS. The following is an example of a completed issue analysis showing total support by each actor and the overall probability of support.

ISSUE: *Restrict the Number of Hospital Beds in the Community*

Actors	Issue Position	X	Power	X	Salience	=	Total Support by Actor
	−3−0−+3		1−3		1−3		
Hospital Administrators	−2	X	2	X	3	=	−12
Community Health Board	0	X	3	X	2	=	(6)
Hospital Staff	−2	X	1	X	3	=	−6
Association of Physicians	−1	X	1	X	2	=	−2
Mass Media	+2	X	2	X	1	=	+4
Citizens Committee	+3	X	1	X	2	=	+6
		X		X		=	
		X		X		=	

Totals: A— Scores of all actors supporting the issue: 10
      B— Absolute value of actors opposing the issue: 20
      C— Scores of actors with zero issue positions: 6
      D—Totals A, B, C: 36
      E— Total A + ½ of Total C: 13
      Probability of Support $= \dfrac{E}{D} = \dfrac{13}{36} = .36$ (36%)

with the positive weights.

5. Divide E, weights in support of the issue, by D, total weights in the system. The resulting figure is the proportion of positive weights in relation to the total weights. This should be understood as the probability that change with regards to the issue will be supported.

Where the probability of support is low (under 50 percent), this means that program change is not likely to be adopted and the project team may have to decide either not to proceed with the program design project or make a special effort to persuade opponents to become supporters. This is the situation in Exhibit 4.2 where the probability of support on the issue of restricting the number of hospital beds in the community is .36 (or 36 percent).

STEP 5—IDENTIFYING STRATEGIES

Having identified political obstacles that may be in the way of achieving program change, the next step is to devise strategies for overcoming them.[3] Here, the team leader, with the assistance of other members of the project team, is expected to perform the role of a political entrepreneur.[4] The basic approach which underlies this role is to change either the issue position, the power status, and/or the salience of the key actors whose support may be necessary to achieve program change. Some general strategies to be considered are as follows:

1. *Persuasion.* The team should consider using arguments of a symbolic or factual nature which may convince opponents to change their mind. This may require showing others that the problem is more serious than they believe. By martialing facts and demonstrating the urgency of the situation, resistors may come to realize the need for program change. Focus especially on the actor that has not yet taken an issue position. Attempt to convince the neutral party that program change on the issue implies at least some changes that will promote the neutral's interests and values.

2. *Bargaining.* Bargaining could be tried as a secondary strategy where persuasion does not work or is insufficient to turn the tide. This method entails sacrificing something of political value in exchange for support. Where bargaining is believed to be necessary, the remaining questions concern what ought to be sacrificed and how much. This means finding out what the other party wants. Generally, there are three types of tradeoffs: concessions on substantive program features during the design phase; nonprogram-related side payments like patronage, public testimonials, or logrolling arrangements; and good will such as an implied obligation to render a favor of some kind in the future.

3. *Mobilizing allies.* Those actors identified as likely to be supportive should be persuaded not only to take a stand but also to exert themselves to win the support of still others. The team leader should consider whether publicity and general commotion will, on balance, create more support for program change than opposition to it. Where publicity to promote saliency is viewed as being advantageous, the mass media could be utilized. A more strategic approach for creating a coalition may be activating the channels of interpersonal communication within the attentive public. This requires enlisting individuals who are actively involved in relevant organizations and are part of the informal system of communications.

4. *Undermining the opposition.* Where techniques of exploiting opportunities and mobilizing allies are insufficient, confrontation and conflict with the opposition may then be unavoidable. This involves undermining the influence of opponents on the issue through various maneuvers that the project team should plan in advance. Examples include routing the proposal away from a decision-making body that is likely to reject it and directing it to another arena where favorable action can be expected, or scheduling hearings, meetings and other events that are likely to work to the advantage of program change. Where it is necessary to escalate the level of conflict, the team should consider attacking the credibility of the opposition's expertise or knowledge with regard to important aspects of the issue. In addition, one can sometimes undermine an adversary by representing it as grossly unfair, illegitimate, or unjustified.

SUMMARY

This chapter has tried to show that program change in the public sector requires public support. Public support doesn't necessarily happen, however, unless it is promoted through various strategies. In light of this, the team leader, with the assistance of other members of the project team, must be willing and able to perform the role of a political entrepreneur. This involves identifying key actors that are likely to influence the program change process. Focusing on issue position, power and salience, an important task is determining how much weight each actor is likely to have and the overall probability of success. When this is determined, the project team should then devise appropriate techniques to diffuse opposition and reinforce support among the actors. Strategies range from opportunity exploiting methods of persuasion and bargaining to the more confrontational methods of mobilizing allies and undermining the opposition.

NOTES

1. See Coplin, William D., and O'Leary, Michael K., *Everyman's Prince, A Guide to Understanding Your Political Problems* (North Scituate, MA: Duxbury Press, 1972); and Coplin, William D., and O'Leary, Michael K., *PS 23: Political Analysis Through the Prince System* (Croton-on-Hudson: Policy Studies Associates, 1983).

2. Coplin and O'Leary, *Political Analysis Through the Prince System.*

3. See Bardach, Eugene, *The Skill Factor in Politics* (Berkeley: University of California Press, 1972).

4. See Moore, Barbara H., ed. *The Entrepreneur in Local Government* (Washington, DC: The International City Management Association, 1983).

CHAPTER 5

PREPARING A WORKPLAN _____

Before a program design project can begin, a workplan should be completed. A workplan serves two basic functions: it provides an overview for all concerned as to what will be involved in the total work effort, and it helps guide the project team in the course of doing the program design. Where there is no workplan, problems in coordination and the misuse of resources in implementing the project are likely to result. Even more damaging is the likelihood that different people will have different interpretations of what the project is all about and what it is supposed to accomplish.

Essentially six steps are involved in preparing a workplan. They are (1) defining the problem that the program is intended to deal with; (2) describing the current program for the purpose of orienting the project team and the decision makers who must approve the workplan; (3) establishing the scope of the project; (4) describing the methods of collecting and organizing the data; (5) establishing and assigning work tasks along with time/effort and cost estimates; and (6) approving the workplan.

The workplan outlined in Exhibit 5.1 specifies the questions to be answered. A formal or informal review by agency personnel and decision makers should take place upon its completion. It is important that local agency officials and the project team agree to the workplan including the scope of the project, the time schedule, dollar costs and what the final product will look like. Any confusion or misunderstanding should be cleared up at this time.

EXHIBIT 5.1. WORKPLAN OUTLINE.

I. Introduction
   A.   What is this document?
   B.   Why has this document been written?
   C.   For whom has this document been prepared?
   D.   What does this document contain?

II. Problem Statement
   A.   What is the problem that the program is intended to deal with?
   B.   What are indicators that show that a problem exists?
   C.   What are the causes of the problem?
   D.   How significant is the problem as determined by the scope (how widespread), by certain impacts, and by the duration (will it persist)?

III. Description of Current Program
   A.   What is the program purpose(s)?
   B.   What is the program background?
   C.   Who are the clients?
   D.   What is the program's funding?
   E.   What does the organizational structure look like?
   F.   How many employees are there and what do they do?
   G.   What are the current operating procedures?
   H.   Are there performance indicators and is there evidence of a performance gap(s)? If so, describe the service deficiency.

IV. Project Scope
   A.   What questions must be answered as determined by the policy makers, top management and/or the project analyst?
   B.   What are the project objectives?
   C.   What is going to be produced in response to the above questions?

V. Project Methodology
   A.   Describe the steps to be taken in
        (1) generating program alternatives, and
        (2) screening program alternatives.
   B.   Describe the steps to be taken in collecting data focusing on:
        (1) service demand, (2) cost, (3) effectiveness, and (4) feasibility.
   C.   Describe how the data will be organized for the purpose of comparing alternatives.

VI. Project Team
   A.   Indicate who will perform specific tasks.
   B.   Proportion of time/effort contributed by the analyst, team leader, and agency personnel.

VII. Work Schedule
   Prepare a work schedule by tasks and steps on a monthly basis as appropriate. (See Exhibit 5.3.)

VIII. Cost Estimate
   Prepare a cost estimate covering labor, overhead, travel, per diem, materials, supplies, and equipment in tabular form.

STEP 1—DEFINING THE PROBLEM

At this stage, the problem that has been selected for analysis must be carefully defined. Initially, the analyst may tend to respond to an issue as perceived by officials, managers, clients or civic leaders. Their definition, however, may be stated vaguely or incorrectly. Where this is so, the analyst should identify indicators that show the extent to which the problem or need exists (e.g., percentage of families classified as poor, or the percentage of workers unemployed). In doing this, it would be helpful to refer back to the first part of Exercise 3.1.

In addition, the analyst should respond to the real problem that underlies an issue; otherwise he or she may be dealing with symptoms. This requires understanding the causes that may be involved and most likely reformulating the problem. It is also necessary to assess the overall significance of the problem by noting who is affected, how widespread it is, and whether the problem is likely to last if no action is taken. To do this, the analyst may have to consult with knowledgeable professionals or experts who have familiarity with the situation. Major changes in the problem statement should be worked out jointly with responsible officials before proceeding with the analysis.[1]

To illustrate, a city mental health department identified a certain neighborhood as having a high proportion of young people between the ages of fifteen to seventeen manifesting a history of drug abuse. The initial problem definition by officials was to relate such drug abuse to inadequate counseling by mental health workers in a local outreach clinic. This definition overlooked the home environment of the clients, particularly conditions of poverty and neglect. The analyst was able to show that the problem of drug abuse was more complex than initially perceived and that a program to deal with the situation necessitated considerations of home conditions. For further instruction on how to develop a problem statement, refer to Exhibit 5.2.

STEP 2—DESCRIBING THE CURRENT PROGRAM

After the problem has been defined, the next step is to describe the current program (or programs) that addresses the problem in order to orient the project team and the decision makers who must approve the workplan. This should cover such features as the program's purpose, background, clientele, funding, organizational structure and procedures, personnel and performance. Questions to be posed to management and staff are listed in the workplan outline in Exhibit 5.1. Particularly important is the need to assess agency performance and to substantiate the extent to which there is evidence of a performance gap. (Refer back to Exercise 3.1.) Holes or gaps that are identified can then be used as a basis for determining the scope of the program design project as described in Step 3 below. Where it is the case that no program addresses the problem directly, the analyst should identify any relevant activities that may address the problem indirectly. Under such circumstances, the performance gap is obvious.

STEP 3—ESTABLISHING THE PROJECT SCOPE

Project scope refers to the particular aspects of the problem that will be addressed as well as to the level of detail. For example, should the analysis focus on very narrow aspects of the problem or should it treat many and broad aspects of the problem? Referring to the earlier illustration of a drug abuse problem among youth, a proposed program could focus on improving the counseling skills of youth workers; or it could enlarge the scope by including counseling of parents as well as youth. The scope could be further widened to include education on drug abuse to local residents to encourage community support.

EXHIBIT 5.2. STEPS IN GENERATING A PROBLEM STATEMENT

Step 1. What problem have you selected for analysis?

Step 2. Check and make certain that the problem is not a symptom of other problems. If you use the word "because" in your problem statement, chances are that everything before "because" is a symptom of the true problem. The problem cited after "because" may actually be the problem statement.

Example: Suppose you have listed the following two statements as the problem that the program addresses:

1. There is a high number of runaways between ages 13 to 18 in the city of Akron because . . .
2. Communications are deficient between adolescents and parents at home.

Depending on the philosophy of the program, statement 1 can be seen as a symptom of statement 2. Now list your problem statement again by referring to statement 2, but recognizing that statement 1 is an indicator of the problem.

Step 3. Identify documentation that indicates the existence of the problem. This can range anywhere from hard data based on a needs assessment or census figures to "expert opinion." Always try to identify the most objective documentation available.

Step 4. Now make sure your problem statement is clear and concise. One way to check this is to ask whether your problem statement can be broken down further into several problem statements. In other words, a problem statement should deal with a single issue. What follows is an example of a problem statement that should be broken down into two statements:

Counselors do not understand the fundamentals of drug abuse and have inadequate counseling skills.

This can be broken down as follows:

1. Counselors do not understand the fundamentals of drug abuse.
2. Counselors have inadequate counseling skills.

SOURCE: Adapted from the National Institute on Drug Abuse, *Prevention Planning Workbook*, Vol. 1. Washington, D.C.: U.S. Government Printing Office, 1981, p. 13.

It is not likely that a program design project could or should focus on all aspects of a problem. How broad an effort should be attempted will be based, for the most part, on the amount of resources and time available to the team as well as the needs and interests of the agency. The analyst must decide within these constraints whether the scope is sufficient to deal with the problem. Where it is defined too narrowly, the proposed project may not significantly affect the problem situation.

A way of dealing with this before the project gets underway is to identify the questions to be answered by the analysis through consultation with relevant decision makers. After these questions are clarified, specific project objectives should be established.

The following questions from the aforementioned drug abuse program serve as useful illustration:

1. How can a drug control program be designed to effectively reduce the number of drug abuse youth in neighborhood X?

2. How can mental health counselors work more effectively with drug abuse youth and their parents?

3. How can an educational program be designed to encourage neighborhood residents and institutions to be supportive of drug abuse clients?

Having formulated the questions, project objectives can be defined as follows:

1. To design more effective drug control counseling to reduce the number of drug abuse youth in neighborhood X.

2. To improve the home environment of drug abuse youth by instituting liaison activities between counselors and the parents of clients.

3. To encourage community support of drug abuse clients through improved education of neighborhood residents about the problem of drug abuse.

The analyst may also find it useful to specify what specifically is going to be produced in response to questions and project objectives. For example, an interim draft report could be produced to allow a midway review by the agency; and subsequently, a final report which would include an executive summary and supporting data.

The scope of the project should be stated in writing in the workplan so that all parties, including the agency, will understand precisely what issues will be addressed and what will be produced before the study actually begins. Questions and objectives should relate directly to what management needs to know to make its decisions. Providing this information in advance will help to prevent after-the-fact misunderstandings about what the project was supposed to accomplish.

STEP 4—DESCRIBING THE PROGRAM METHODOLOGY

Identifying appropriate information sources and data collection methods is the key to a successful program design. Where the methodology is ill-conceived or the data is poor, the analysis on which the program design is based will have little or no validity. In doing a workplan, the analyst must think through in advance what kinds of data will be needed, whether it is available and how to collect it. There are generally three prime considerations in defining the methodology.

First, the analyst should identify procedures for generating new alternatives and subsequently, screening them. Most important is the need to identify sources to be investigated to develop ideas for program alternatives. Knowledgeable officials, agency personnel, other jurisdictions, and organizations that specialize in the program area are appropriate sources of information. In addition, brainstorming with colleagues and other informed individuals is a technique that often proves highly useful. The analyst should consider carefully those particular sources in Exhibit 7.1 (Chapter Seven) which could be utilized. See, also, Exercise 7.1 on brainstorming.[2]

A second consideration pertains to the types of data to be collected to support the analysis. Estimates should be made of the expected service demand for each alternative, how much each alternative is likely to cost, how effective each alternative is likely to be, and the feasibility of each alternative. The analyst should explain how he or she will make these estimates. Exhibits 8.1 to 8.5 in Chapter Eight should be referred to for a description of particular strategies that could be used.[3]

Third, the analyst must anticipate how the data is to be organized in order to compare alternatives for the purpose of selecting the one or two likely to return the most benefits with the least costs. (See Chapter Nine.) Where there is more than one issue being considered, then each issue should be analyzed and an alternative recommended along with supporting data.

STEP 5—ESTABLISHING AND ASSIGNING WORK TASKS

As previously discussed, the project team may consist of a team leader, an agency staff person, and the analyst. To implement the workplan, team personnel should be assigned their roles or work tasks on the basis of the list of work elements specified below. (See Exhibit 5.3 for an illustration.) The list is not intended to be definitive and will vary somewhat as conditions and expectations vary.

1. Orient the agency to the analysis effort.
2. Prepare a flow chart or schematic diagram of all activities involved in an ongoing program.
3. Coordinate team work assignments.
4. Clarify goals and generate program alternatives.
5. Determine data requirements.
6. Determine data availability.
7. Gather data.
8. Analyze data.
9. Prepare a draft report.
10. Review the draft report with the agency affected and relevant citizen or client groups.
11. Prepare the final report.
12. Present the results of the project.

To the extent it is possible to do so, estimates should be made of the time and effort that will be contributed by each of the participants. (See Exhibit 5.4.) It should be recognized that

EXHIBIT 5.3 WORK SCHEDULE. *Family Life Education Project*

	Phase I			Phase II		Phase III	Phase IV
Task and Assignment	Jan	Feb	Mar	Apr	May	Jun	Jul
1. Identify needs (Analyst)	—	—					
2. Orient agency (Team Leader)		—					
3. Develop team (Team Leader)		—					
4. Establish program goals (Analyst & Team)			—				
5. Generate alternatives (Analyst & Team)			—				
6. Determine data requirements (Analyst & Financial Adviser)			—				
7. Collect data (Analyst, Team & Financial Adviser)				—			
8. Analyze data (Analyst, Team & Financial Adviser)				—			
9. Prepare findings/draft report (Analyst)					—		
10. Present draft to Executive Director/Family Life Education Committee for feedback (Team Leader)					—		
11. Prepare final report (Analyst)						—	
12. Present to Executive Director and Family Education Committee (Team Leader)						—	
13. Family Life Education Committee Chairman presents to Board for action						—	

EXHIBIT 5.4. ESTIMATES OF TIME AND EFFORT. *Family Life Education Project*

	Phase I	Phase II	Phase III	Phase IV
Team Leader	4 hrs/wk X 2 wks	10 hrs/wk X 8 wks	8 hrs/wk X 3 wks	3 hrs/wk X 2 wks
		8 + 80 + 24 + 6 = 118 hours		
2 Team Members (Total)	— — — —	24 hrs/wk X 7 wks	16 hrs/wk X 3 wks	— — — — —
		168 + 48 = 216 hours		
Program Analyst	8 hrs/wk X 8 wks	16 hrs/wk X 8 wks	24 hrs/wk X 3 wks	6 hrs/wk X 2 wks
		64 + 128 + 72 + 12 = 276 hours		
Financial Adviser	— — — —	2 hrs/wk X 2 wks	4hrs/wk X 6 wks	— — — — —

the time required will vary substantially depending on the size and complexity of the program and the manpower available to the project team. Each task could take from a few hours to several months depending upon the circumstances. Cost estimates should then be made covering labor, overhead, travel, per diem, materials, supplies and equipment in tabular form.

STEP 6—APPROVING THE WORKPLAN

The completed workplan should be presented to the program agency and participating officials so that everyone involved fully understands and endorses the project before it begins. Tradeoffs can be made at this time with respect to scope, time-span, resources and technical rigor. For example, management may agree to eliminating one or more steps in order to have the project completed earlier than projected, or they may wish to commit more resources to widen the scope. Any changes made should be put in writing to avoid after-the-fact misunderstandings.

This does not mean, however, that the project cannot be altered after work commences. The project team may find that important data are not available or that unexpected delays necessitate more funds than initially expected. When circumstances cause unanticipated change in the project, the team leader should discuss such change with management and officials to establish a new understanding of what is to be accomplished. Under no circumstances should the project team make unilateral decisions which change the scope of the project.

SUMMARY

An important task to be completed at the beginning of the program design project is the preparation of a workplan. The workplan serves to guide the project team by defining the scope of the project, specifying information sources and data collection methods, and assigning tasks to appropriate individuals. Thus everyone knows ahead of time what is to be involved with few unexpected surprises along the way; this helps to avoid many unnecessary delays and errors. Another related benefit is that the workplan serves to reduce misunderstandings and conflicting expectations among those that have a stake in the final product.

NOTES

1. A useful discussion of problem definitions is to be found in Zaltman and Duncan, *Strategies for Planned Changes*, pp. 32–58. For a discussion of the context of problem recognition, see, Brewer, Garry D. and deLeon, Peter, *The Foundations of Policy Analysis* (Homewood, IL: The Dorsey Press, 1983). pp. 35–60.

2. A useful overview of methods of finding and screening alternatives is to be found in Quade, *Analysis for Public Decisions*, pp. 107–112. See, also, Delbecq, Andres L., et al., *Group Techniques for Program Planning: A Guide to Nominal Group and Delphi Processes* (Glenview, IL: Scott, Foresman and Co., 1975).

3. Quade, *Analysis for Public Decisions*, pp. 113–116.

ESTABLISHING GOALS, OBJECTIVES AND PERFORMANCE CRITERIA _____

Though they can be difficult to find, public service programs usually have statements which describe their goals and objectives. A program goal can be defined as a broad statement of purpose or intended achievement as established by policy makers or high ranking administrators. A program objective can be defined as a more specific statement of intent that serves to achieve a stated goal. Program objectives are usually established by agency administrators and their staffs. An illustration of a statement of goals and objectives for a drug abuse program can be seen in Exhibit 6.1.

Program goals and objectives are important for the following reasons. First, it tells program personnel where they should be going. Where clearly defined goals and objectives are not available, there is no sound basis for designing a program. If you don't know where you are going, it is difficult to select a means of getting there. A second important reason for stating goals and objectives is that it enables the agency to estimate whether the intent of the program can be accomplished and, once the program is underway, whether it is being accomplished. As we shall see, criteria for making such an assessment are derived directly from the goals and objectives. A third reason is that a statement of goals and objectives makes it possible for citizens and clients to know whether the program is meeting their needs. Where objectives are understood, citizens and clients are better able to decide which program activities are helping them and which ones are expendable.

Where the benefits of having clear and precise program goals and objectives are not understood or appreciated by agency personnel, the analyst must provide necessary assistance. In most cases, he or she may do nothing more than make sure that goals and objectives are available and current. In situations where a new program is being established, the analyst may have to participate in a goal- and objective-setting process. Generally, goals and objectives can be derived from program documentation already in existence. The steps outlined below are intended to provide guidance on how to proceed. They are (1) reviewing program material, (2) defining program goals, (3) defining objectives, and (4) establishing performance criteria.

STEP 1 — REVIEWING PROGRAM MATERIAL

As a first step, the analyst must examine source material which pertains to the program in order to get a general understanding of the basic purpose of the program. This was previously called for in developing the workplan. However, the need for greater precision at this stage may require more intensive efforts through a search of some or all of the following sources.

The agency budget. The program agency's annual budget will often have statements of program goals and objectives as justification for funding requests.

Program personnel. Personnel usually have knowledge of the program history and operations. In addition, they usually have access to records containing information on policy and specific objectives which are based on that policy. Program personnel can also reveal which goals and objectives are realistically being pursued and which ones are being ignored.

Legislation and legal documents. An examination of relevant statutes and legal documents will often convey understanding of the intent and scope of the program.

Statements and messages of elected officials, board members, citizens. Formal messages, speeches, and testimony before committees which pertain to the creation, expansion, or abolition of a program may convey insights into the implied objectives of the program.

Minutes of oversight body. Many service programs have some body such as the city council or a board or commission which provides review and direction. The minutes or annual reports of such bodies should be examined for insights.

STEP 2 — DEFINING PROGRAM GOALS

A program goal describes in general terms what it is that the program should accomplish. It should be written according to the following criteria:[1]

—A goal covers relatively long term spans;

—A goal should be client- or citizen-oriented;

—A goal should not predetermine the details of program activities;

—A goal should be expressed as a desired outcome to be achieved rather than as an action or a process;

—A goal should reflect the direction desired by policy makers and top administrators, not staff personnel.

Examples of program goal statements are:

Preventive health care: To provide long-term medical care for low-income families so as to avoid serious health problems.

Services for the elderly: To upgrade the service-provider skills of home volunteers so as to improve the living conditions of the elderly.

Foster care: To place all foster children in a safe and stable environment to which they can adjust and where they will not be neglected.

Crime control: To assure the security and safety of citizens through more effective policing.

If the analyst cannot find a statement of program goals, then it is necessary to begin anew through a goal-setting process. Where there are constraints of time, however, this may be difficult to do. The most expeditious strategy is for the analyst to work with the head of the agency for the purpose of drafting a goals statement which is then presented to top managers and board members as a basis for discussion. Policy makers are more likely to take an interest if they can be impressed with the importance of goals for the efficient and effective management of public service programs.[2]

STEP 3—DEFINING PROGRAM OBJECTIVES

Objectives are derived from goals, but because they are much more specific than goals, objectives may be more difficult to formulate. In defining an objective, the following should be kept in mind:[3]

—An objective must be accomplished in order to achieve a goal;

—An objective should be expressed as a desired outcome rather than an action or a process;

—An objective should speak to the needs of clients or citizens;

—An objective should account for unintended or negative effects.

Exhibit 6.1 presents examples of objectives as derived from a particular goal. If objectives are not clear from available sources, the analyst will have to define them in close consultation with program personnel. Even where sources are available, they may be dated since programs tend to change with time. In such cases they may have to be redefined. The objectives used should be those that program personnel agree are appropriate.

EXHIBIT 6.1. PROGRAM OBJECTIVES. Below are examples of program objectives determined according to the guidelines presented in Step 3.

Goal: To reduce drug abuse through improved treatment of clients.
Objectives:

1. To maintain a monthly average of 230 clients receiving services.
2. To maintain an average of 30 clients per day in residential treatment.
3. To reduce the number of reentries by 50% in 1981 below the total reentries in 1980.
4. To insure that 60% of all persons discharged will be sound and drug free.
5. To provide vocational and job development training that will result in 11% of the clients being given successful job placements.
6. To provide a minimum of 1,000 referral services.
7. To have 50% of the total clients as new clients for treatment.

Exercises 6.1 and 6.2

Viewing your own program, the reader should now test his or her skill in formulating objectives by answering the questions in Exercise 6.1. In most cases, you will not be able to provide all the answers by yourself and should use the questions to interview persons who are involved with the program. Of importance here is the need to consider the potential effects of objectives on various clientele groups. Different groups are likely to be affected in different ways. For example, the placing of physical barriers around buildings as a crime prevention measure may benefit the general population but pose a special burden on the free movement of the handicapped. To illustrate further, groups such as youth and the elderly have distinct needs in the areas of health and the family. How they are likely to be affected by a program must be estimated separately from effects on the typical adult. It is necessary, therefore, to identify measures and collect information which show how the program is likely to impact each group. Especially important are unintended negative effects. Where certain effects are likely to be harmful to a particular group, the program objective should be reconsidered. The preparation of a clientele group profile, specifying different characteristics, will help the reader anticipate different kinds of impacts. The reader should identify clientele groups by using the classification scheme in Exercise 6.2. Generally, information can be obtained through agency records or census data.

The list of program objectives defined by the analyst should be approved by the agency head before it is sent on to top management. In most cases, policy officials are not involved in objective-setting since they get involved on a broader level through goal-setting. Special care should be taken to assure that objectives that have been identified are still relevant and have bearing on the future development of activities.

STEP 4—ESTABLISHING PERFORMANCE CRITERIA

After program objectives have been agreed to, performance criteria must be defined for each objective.[4] This serves two purposes. First, the analyst must be able to estimate how well different program alternatives are likely to achieve the stated objectives. Alternatives that are not likely to be very effective should be discarded. Without clear criteria, estimates of effectiveness cannot be made. (This is discussed in greater detail in the next chapter.) Second, once program alternatives have been selected, performance criteria are used to assess progress toward the objectives in the implementation stage.

In establishing performance criteria, the following considerations apply:
—Criteria should be based on services provided for people being served;
—Criteria should be based on specific performance targets;
—Criteria should be objective;
—Criteria should indicate degrees of accomplishment;
—Criteria should be agreed to by major actors involved in the program—managers, supervisors, field personnel.

Exhibit 6.2 illustrates performance criteria based on objectives presented in Exhibit 6.1. Before turning to Exhibit 6.2, however, the reader should attempt to define criteria using the

EXERCISE 6.1. IDENTIFYING YOUR PROGRAM OBJECTIVES

1. What is the purpose of the program, both in the short-run and the long-run? How does the program manager know if it is working? What evidence is utilized as indicating success?

2. What are possible side effects from this program, both in the short-run and the long-run? What are the negative aspects? What are the positive aspects?

3. Who is the program's clientele? What types of people? How large is this group? Where are they located? Who else might be affected unintentionally?

4. What would be the consequences if the program was eliminated? What would happen to the clientele or citizens being served?

SOURCE: Adapted from Public Technology, Inc., *Program Evaluation and Analysis*. Washington, DC: U.S. Department of Housing and Urban Development, Nov. 1978, p. 15.

EXERCISE 6.2. CLASSIFYING PROGRAM CLIENTELE

Use the following criteria to classify clientele being impacted.

1. Residence location—Grouped by neighborhood, service area, precinct, etc., for local governments or by county, region, planning district, etc., for states.

2. Sex.

3. Age—Such groups as youth and elderly may have particular needs relevant to certain programs.

4. Family income groups—Often the poor have special needs.

5. Racial/ethnic groups.

6. Special handicapped groups.

7. Education level.

8. Home ownership and type of dwelling.

9. Employment status.

10. Family size.

SOURCE: Adapted from Public Technology, Inc., *Program Evaluation and Analysis.* Washington, DC: U.S. Department of Housing and Urban Development, Nov. 1978, p. 15.

same objectives in Exhibit 6.1. After you've done this, compare the criteria that you have selected with those in Exhibit 6.2. It should not be expected that your criteria will exactly match those to be found in Exhibit 6.2, as different persons will project different interests and perspectives in the course of defining criteria. Where there are significant differences, which ones are more appropriate as based on the considerations discussed above?

In viewing Exhibit 6.2, note that multiple criteria may be defined for an objective. Generally, it is better to have more than one criterion to better assure validity. As previously mentioned, there is no right or wrong value for each criterion. The number of clients receiving services per month can be compared with the number of clients of other agencies or national averages, but no ideal standard exists. Such criteria are usually intended as indicators of performance, i.e., as performance targets to estimate and subsequently assess progress. While objective criteria are preferred because they assure greater validity in measuring performance, subjective criteria could also be used. For example, there is growing emphasis in many service agencies on citizen or client perceptions of quality of services delivered as discerned through sample surveys. Certainly the degree of citizen or client satisfaction with agency services is too critical an indicator to be ignored.

EXHIBIT 6.2. PERFORMANCE CRITERIA. This example shows performance criteria for the objectives developed in Exhibit 6.1. The criteria adhere to the guidelines presented in Step 4.

Goal: To reduce drug abuse through improved treatment of clients.

Objectives:	*Performance Criteria:*
1. To maintain a monthly average 230 clients receiving services.	1. Average number of clients per month.
2. To maintain an average of 30 clients per day in residential treatment.	2. Average number of residential treatment clients per day.
3. To reduce the number of re-entries by 50% in 1981 below the total reentries of 1980.	3. Percentage reduction of re-entries.
4. To insure that 60% of all persons discharged will be sound and drug free.	4a. Percentage of drug free persons discharged. b. Clients sense of well-being—good, moderate, low by %.
5. To provide vocational and job development training that will result in 11% of the clients being given successful job placements.	5a. Percentage of clients given successful job placements. b. Percentage of placed clients satisfied with jobs. c. Percentage who hold jobs beyond first 6 months.
6. To provide a minimum of 1,000 referral services.	6. Number of referrals provided.
7. To have 50% of the total clients new clients for treatment.	7. Percentage of new clients.

SUMMARY

Based on the rational model of problem solving, this chapter has emphasized the importance of clarifying the goals and objectives for the program being designed. Where goals and objectives are poorly defined, or where they do not exist, they must be developed anew. This is because they specify the purposes of the program—i.e., what will the program try to achieve? They also help in estimating how difficult it may be to attain the purposes of the program. After objectives have been defined, performance criteria must be established for each objective. As demonstrated in Chapters Seven and Eight that follow, such criteria provide specific indices by which to measure progress toward the objectives and they help the analyst estimate and compare how well different program alternatives are likely to achieve the stated objectives.

NOTES

1. For a useful elaboration on defining goals, see Mager, Robert F., *Goal Analysis* (Belmont, CA: Fearon Pitman, 1972).

2. See Rothman, Jack, et al., *Promoting Innovation and Change in Organizations and Communities* (New York: John Wiley & Sons, Inc., 1976) pp. 59–93.

3. For a useful elaboration on defining objectives, see Mager, Robert F., *Preparing Instructional Objectives* (Belmont, CA: Fearon Pitman, 1975).

4. For illustrations in different service areas, see Hatry, Harry P., et al., *How Effective Are Your Community Services?* (Washington, DC: The Urban Institute and the International City Management Association, 1977).

CHAPTER 7

DEVELOPING PROGRAM
ALTERNATIVES _____

When the initial steps of selecting a problem area, preparing a workplan, and defining goals, objectives and performance criteria have been completed, the project team may proceed to the program design stage. This chapter focuses on what is probably the most critical phase of the program design project—the development of program alternatives. Where the project team fails to be enterprising and imaginative in carrying out this task, the end results are likely to be disappointing.

Four basic steps are involved. The first two are generating alternatives and then screening them to identify the most promising ones. In doing this, however, the analyst and project team must be future oriented which requires a third step: forecasting conditions of some future point in time that would influence the selection of alternatives. The fourth step consists of categorizing alternatives that have been identified by the degree to which they depart from the existing program which is the basis for anticipating how difficult it may be for estimating costs and effectiveness in the subsequent stages of analysis.

STEP 1—GENERATING PROGRAM ALTERNATIVES

The entire project team should participate in the process of generating alternatives. It is important that all team members understand the goals, objectives, and performance criteria that have been formulated for the program; otherwise the alternatives identified are not likely to be appropriate for the achievement of those goals and objectives.

56

A critical aspect in the development of alternatives is the kind of effort the project team makes in searching for new and different approaches. Decision makers often have preconceived notions about ways to approach particular problems and are sometimes reluctant to engage in serious examination of available sources.[1] Where this is the case, the best possible alternatives will not be identified. A concerted effort should be made to consult with others on the basis of their ability to contribute in special ways, for example, officials, program agency personnel and other groups and organizations that have had experience with particular programs. Some typical information sources are described in Exhibit 7.1. Refer also to Appendices A, B and C.

Exercise 7.1

It may be useful to conduct 'brainstorming' sessions involving the project team, agency personnel and other knowledgeable persons to generate ideas. Such sessions could produce more imaginative proposals than would otherwise be forthcoming. Exercise 7.1 shows how the technique of brainstorming may be used to best advantage. The reader is encouraged to perform the exercise with approximately three to eight persons; it may also be used as a classroom activity where students are divided into small groups organized around specific projects.[2]

EXERCISE 7.1. BRAINSTORMING

Using a small group of about three to eight colleagues, the following procedures should be used in brainstorming a problem.

1. First, brainstorm the problem according to the following rules:
   a. Seek ideas, not critical analysis. All critical judgment should be ruled out.
   b. All kinds of ideas should be encouraged in the spontaneity which comes when judgment is suspended. Practical considerations are not important at this point.
   c. The more ideas produced, the better. At this point, quality considerations should be suspended.
   d. Where possible, build on the ideas of other brainstormers. List ideas below.

2. Second, apply critical judgment to the ideas proposed.
   a. Team members should review proposed ideas by applying their best judgment. How appropriate are they in light of organizational factors?
   b. Seek clues for something sound in even the strangest ideas.
   c. Arrange ideas in priority order for presentation to decision makers.

STEP 2—SCREENING PROGRAM ALTERNATIVES

After a range of possible alternatives have been identified, the project team should review them for the purpose of selecting three to six of the most promising ones. A useful method in the screening process is the preparation of a description of each alternative or set of related alternatives. This should follow a standard format so that alternatives can be subsequently compared on the basis of estimated costs, effectiveness and feasibility. Exhibit 7.2 presents a sample description of a plan to attack excessive vandalism thought to be related to alcohol abuse. The overall goal of the program is to control vandalism by making changes in the environment or places that youth between the ages of thirteen and seventeen spend a majority of their time. The alternatives proposed are the establishment of a street academy and job training and referral. As the exhibit shows, program objectives and program elements are translated into relevant measures so that the analyst and the agency staff can judge the program's progress.

EXHIBIT 7.1. SOURCES FOR PROGRAM ALTERNATIVES. The list below suggests some of the sources that an analyst should investigate to develop ideas for program alternatives.

Board Members and Officials. Program changes are often initiated in response to a specific request by ranking officials. They will usually indicate alternatives that they want included in the analysis.

Agency Personnel. Personnel of the program agency may be able to recommend alternatives based on their experiences in a service providing capacity, knowledge of what other agencies are doing, or current concepts and theories that they are familiar with.

Professional Associations. Professional associations often serve as a forum for the exchange of information useful for program development. This is accomplished through such means as publications, conferences, training and consultation. Listings of associations with addresses are provided in Appendix A and B.

Community-Based Groups. Community organizations, the news media, labor unions, business groups, public interest organizations, and concerned citizens may have ideas to propose. These sources may not only volunteer information, but often reflect vested interests and assert pressure to initiate program modification.

Clearinghouse Services. Upon request, search services will scan relevant literature and data banks and send back abstracts and other references. A listing of services with addresses is provided in Appendix C.

Team Brainstorming. Groups sessions may be devoted to the production of possible alternatives. For illustration of a structured approach to brainstorming, refer to Exercise 7.1. This method explicitly strives to generate new alternatives that have not been tried before.

The Existing Program. Increasing or decreasing the scope of the present program may also be considered as alternatives. This could include the effects of discontinuing the program altogether.

After the alternatives have been described, the project team should consult with management officials to begin eliminating alternatives that do not appear to be feasible. When only two or three alternatives have been generated, screening will not be necessary; however, descriptions should still be presented to serve as a guide for the collection of data that is discussed in the next chapter.

The process of preparing descriptions should help the analyst become aware of other possible approaches and provoke further inquiry. Additional modifications may be necessary and the analyst should not hesitate to continue the search by communicating with leading experts, making phone calls to other jurisdictions and through visitations. Any additional alternatives generated at this stage should also be screened.

STEP 3 — FORECASTING

How effective an alternative is likely to be depends both on the properties of the alternative and on the situation or environment that exists when the alternative is made operational some time in the future. In social services, for example, the residential distribution of clients in a locality will significantly affect how services are delivered. Some neighborhoods will have more elderly persons while others will have a high proportion of families with young children. Therefore, it is necessary to predict changing residential patterns in order to be able to target services more directly to such groupings. Moreover, some alternatives that seem appropriate in light of present conditions may have to be rejected upon projecting future conditions. Changing patterns in the economy, energy sources, the natural environment, life styles, social values and politics are examples of other factors to be considered in predicting the likely effects of proposed alternatives.

Forecasting should take place either concurrently with the generation of alternatives or during the screening process. Methods of forecasting range from computer simulation models to various statistical techniques depending on the subject area and the kind of technical capabilities that are available. In the general area of public services, forecasting is usually done through scenario writing. A scenario can be defined as a description of the basic characteristics of the future context in which alternatives are to be implemented. It involves estimating a sequence of events that is likely to lead from the present time to the scenario. This is demonstrated through the following exercise.

Exercise 7.2

Referring to the diagram in Exercise 7.2, identify the five most important events, developments or trends likely to impact the problem area being analyzed over the next decade. List them in sequential order. On the basis of these factors, describe a scenario that best portrays the future context in which identified alternatives are to function. This should be done through a team effort involving other informed individuals. When done in a group context, such a process helps to clarify the particular assumptions that underlie a forecast. In addition, it forces the analyst to imagine alternative events and conditions that might other-

EXHIBIT 7.2. DESCRIPTION OF A PROGRAM ALTERNATIVE. The following demonstrates how to describe a program alternative using the example of vandalism caused by alcohol-abusing youth. This example includes two related alternatives.

	Relevant Description	Relevant Measures
Problem symptoms	Unacceptable vandalism rate in East End of city	No. & % increase of incidents
Program	Youth Development and Environmental Alcohol Education Program	
Program Objectives	Refer 50 alcohol-abusing vandals to job training or job placement	Reduction in level of unemployment
	Engage 50 alcohol-abusing vandals in environmental alcohol education to reduce abusive behavior	Reduction in level of alcohol-abusing behavior
	Reduce youthful loitering rate by 90%	Reduction in level of loitering
	Reduce vandalism rate to below or equal to the rest of the city within two years and rehabilitate 30% of known vandals within six months of program startup	Reduction in level of vandalism
Program Alternatives	Street academy to address substandard recreation facilities and social and psychological environment of vandals	
	Job referral to address long-term economic, social, and environmental well-being of vandals	

Program Elements	Recreational facilities preparation	Facilities prepared and equipped
	Staff development	Aids trained
	Provision of supportive services	Vandals referred
	Counseling services	Vandals counseled
	Community social services resource group	Regularity of meetings and attendance

Procedures: Define success for each participant based upon a diagnostic inventory of what his/her individual problem areas are. Be responsible for aiding the success of each participant in his/her areas of need.

Encourage peer-group identification, peer counseling, and peer-group responsibility.

Offer late and weekend hours in addition to 5:00 p.m. to 8:00 p.m. after-school hours.

Offer the participant positive and constructive experiences in sorting out problems whether they be of family, school, legal, or other nature. Include such problem-solving skills as problem identification, development of alternative approaches, placing the problem in personal perspective, making commitments to a solution, and setting target dates to achieve these.

Develop community resources that reach out to the participant. Contact community leaders in political, religious, social, and economic organizations. Establish liaison for each participant.

Provide training capability that enables community people to deal with the problems that need to be solved. This will allow for increased use of minimum-level trained, volunteer staff.

Develop a social services resource group composed of representatives of the community and a coalition of program contacts (social service personnel, public health personnel, school personnel, probation officers, employment official). Monthly meetings should be scheduled to foster coordination.

Sponsoring agency: Community Mental Health Department

Required personnel: 1 director, 1 counselor

Location: Colonial Place Health and Recreation Center

SOURCE: Adapted from the National Institute on Alcohol Abuse and Alcoholism, *A Guidebook for Planning Alcohol Prevention Programs With Black Youth.* Washington, DC: U.S. Government Printing Office, 1981, pp. 47, 48.

wise be ignored. Where appropriate, the analyst should revise alternatives to better accommodate particular aspects of the scenario.[3]

EXERCISE 7.2. FORECASTING A SCENARIO

Identify the five most important events, developments or trends likely to impact the problem area over the next decade. List these in sequential order below.

1.

2.

3.

4.

5.

Describe scenario (5 to 10 years from now):

STEP 4—CATEGORIZING ALTERNATIVES

After alternatives have been generated, screened, and forecast, it would be useful to categorize them by type, ranging from those that represent no change from the existing program to new programs with new concepts. The extent to which any particular alternative or set of alternatives departs from the existing program will have a bearing on the subsequent tasks of estimating the costs and effectiveness of alternatives. Thus, the analyst can get a preliminary view of how difficult it will be in completing the analysis. Alternatives can be categorized into five types as presented below.[4]

(1) *Present program extended at the same level of effort.* Here, the existing program is extended into the future with no notable change. This can serve as a baseline for comparing other alternatives. Where data on past costs and performance are available, the tasks of estimating future costs and effectiveness usually pose minimal difficulty.

(2) *Present program extended at a different level of effort.* This type of an alternative represents the continuation of the existing program but with either a higher or lower level of resources. A proposed increase in the number of part-time workers, or a plan to reduce the number of firemen assigned to the night shift are two illustrations. While the costs for more or fewer personnel can usually be estimated without much difficulty, it cannot be assumed that effectiveness will increase or decrease proportionate to the changed level of effort. For example, the effects of reducing the number of firemen on the night shift may be so marginal that it would be very difficult to detect. Effects may be substantial, however, where the neighborhood environment consists of deteriorating slum housing.

(3) *Variations in present program procedures.* This type refers to a change in the method of operations rather than in the level of operations. To illustrate: A school for the handicapped may wish to consider revising certain parts of its curriculum to encourage greater self-reliance for physically-impaired children. A child welfare agency may propose using volunteers to provide certain services to clients to free-up professional personnel to undertake other more critical activities. A health department may decide to modify training of food inspectors to deal more effectively with the problem of food contamination. Estimating costs and effectiveness in such cases is likely to be more difficult than in cases of the previous types. However, the analyst can usually use data that are available for the current program as a first step.

(4) *New programs with traditional concepts.* Where proposed changes in existing program activities become so substantial, they may no longer be considered variations of an existing program. For example, a manpower retraining agency may wish to establish two neighborhood-based training schools with the intent of transporting clients to both schools. The agency never tried this before, but because it is based on a well-established practice, it could be considered an alternative that is of a traditional form. In estimating costs and effectiveness for this type, reference cannot be made to an existing program. However, estimates can be based on the experiences of other jurisdictions that have implemented similar programs.

(5) *New programs with new concepts.* This refers to alternatives that represent new methods that have not been tried before and are nontraditional. An example is the proposed rehabilitation of the mentally ill by taking them out of institutions and locating them as small group living units in the community. Another example is a proposal to allow college students to earn a degree through home-study without the traditional requirement of school attendance. Such alternatives pose the greatest difficulty in estimating costs and effectiveness primarily because they are new and untested. Nor is it likely that other jurisdictions would have much experience with them as a source of data. Sometimes, small pilot tests of such alternatives are a good way of getting information before committing sizeable resources.

SUMMARY

The identification of alternatives is probably the most critical phase of a program design project. If a serious search is not conducted and screening is haphazard, then the alternatives that are finally identified are not likely to be very successful in the attainment of goals and objectives. In addition, the analyst must develop some sense of future conditions for the time that the alternatives are to become operational; where possible changes in the environment are not accounted for, seemingly sound programs could have detrimental effects. Finally, alternatives that have been generated should be reviewed to determine how difficult it might be to assess costs and effectiveness in the next stage of analysis. Otherwise the analyst may underestimate the kind of effort that will be required for completing the project.

NOTES

1. For an elaboration on constraints in the consideration of alternatives, see Kahn, H., and Mann, I., *Ten Common Pitfalls* (Santa Monica, CA: The Rand Corporation, RM-1937, July 1957); cited in Quade; "Pitfalls and Limitations," in Quade, E. S., and Boucher, W. I., eds., *Systems Analysis and Policy Planning: Applications in Defense* (New York: American Elsevier, 1968), p. 351.

2. Other comparable methods are discussed in Coke, James G. and Moore, Carl M., *Guide for Leader Using Nominal Group Technique* (Columbus, Ohio: Academy for Contemporary Problems, 1979); Delbecq, Andres L., et al., *Group Techniques for Program Planning: A Guide to Nominal Group and Delphi Processes* (Glenview, IL: Scott, Foresman and Company, 1975). Also see Parnes, Sidney J., "Do You Really Understand Brainstorming?" in Parnes, S.J., and Harding, H. F., eds., *A Source Book for Creative Thinking* (N.Y.: Charles Scribner's Sons, 1962).

3. See, also, Ascher, William. *Forecasting* (Baltimore, MD: John Hopkins University Press, 1978), pp. 190-214; Duncan, Otis D., "Social Forecasting: The State of the Art," *Public Interest*, Fall 1969, pp. 88-118; Shubik, Martin, "Symposium: The Nature and Limitations of Forecasting," *Daedalus*, Summer, 1967, pp. 938-46.

4. This is developed and illustrated in Hatry, Harry, et al., *Program Analysis for State and Local Government*, pp. 51-55.

CHAPTER 8

DATA COLLECTION _____

At this point in the program design project, the analyst should have identified approximately three to six alternatives that appear to have the most promise for the attainment of program goals and objectives and ultimately the resolution of the problem. In order to be able to make a final recommendation, each alternative must now be carefully examined through the collection of data that address the following: (1) service demand, (2) costs, (3) effectiveness, and (4) feasibility. Each of these is discussed below as a distinct step. The reader should be reminded that this task can be more challenging than might appear to be the case at first glance. This is because the alternative or combination of alternatives to be selected must operate some time in the future; therefore, data must be based on estimates of future conditions rather than simply the present.

STEP 1—ESTIMATING SERVICE DEMAND

The first question to be considered in examining an alternative is how much service should be provided by that alternative. This is because too much of a service beyond demand or need will unnecessarily increase costs, while insufficient service will seriously limit effectiveness and feasibility. Furthermore, some alternatives will be better able to deliver the appropriate amount of services than others.

Where time and skills are available, it is important to get the best possible data on which to estimate service levels. The analyst should try to generate data that will give some indication of expressed demand (which is based on past usage of a service) and latent or hidden demand (which is the demand likely to occur as services become available and people find out about them).

Exhibit 8.1 describes some standard sources for getting information on which to estimate the future demand for a particular service.[1] The analyst should collect data covering a number of past years in order to determine if a trend exists on which to project future demand. Since it is difficult to estimate future demand, particularly when new programs are involved, the analyst may wish to make two or three estimates for different levels of service. This could show how costs and effectiveness are likely to vary as service levels vary. In addition, service demand estimates could be projected over a period of years to show short-term and long-terms costs and effects. With such information available, decision makers will be better able to judge how much of a service they want to provide over time.

EXHIBIT 8.1.—SOURCES FOR DEMAND ESTIMATES. Below are suggested sources for data to estimate the future demand for a particular service.

Data on the current and past incidence of problems. For example, incidence of diseases, incidence of poverty, the crime rate, the rate of illiteracy, the rate of children with physical handicaps.

Demographic data. This may include the number of people of a certain age, sex, residential location, or family income. These raw numbers may be of considerable importance for some services. For example, the number of residences in an area helps determine the need for educational, recreational or health services. In other cases, this information can be used with other information such as incidence rates. For example, the rate of physical handicaps in children between ages one and five might be multiplied by the number of children of those ages in a given area to yield an estimate of the number of children likely to need physical therapy.

Technical assessments of conditions. For example, water and air quality tests, ratings by trained observers of the cleanliness of eating establishments, and health examination surveys. Such assessments can help identify significant problems.

Data on past expressed demand. For example, attendance at recreational facilities, number of persons using health centers or hospitals, and the number of persons applying for program assistance. Waiting lists can also provide a rough estimate of current unmet needs. Many potential clients may not be on such lists, however, while some who are on the lists may not qualify for services.

Citizen or client surveys. For example, a survey asking how many days a person was unable to work for health reasons in the recent past would indicate the magnitude of health problems. Questions about whether clients would use a particular service if offered, or if a present service were changed, can help estimate latent demand.

Complaint data. The number of complaints received about a service can serve as an indication of how well the current demand is being met.

After the service level of each alternative is estimated, the analyst should next estimate costs. To do this, each alternative must be described in sufficient detail so that the proposed activities which comprise each alternative, and the resources to support those activities, are fully accounted for. This is demonstrated in Exhibit 8.2 which shows a completed resource analysis worksheet. On the top of the work sheet is a space to identify the objective which is being analysed. In the first column, activities for objectives are listed. This should be based on the description of the alternative(s) intended to achieve the objective as illustrated in Exhibit 7.2 in the previous chapter. In the second column, resources are listed that will be needed to complete the activity covering the number of people, the skills, the money, and other materials required. More resources will be required where service demand is expected to be high. Resources that are actually available are listed in the third column. Discrepancies between columns 2 and 3 are identified in column 4. Space is available in the fifth column for any notes or comments with regard to each activity. Where discrepancies exist between resources available and resources needed, it may be necessary to restructure the activity so that the unavailable resources are no longer needed; or the activity may have to be dropped which may mean redefining the program objective. The project team could also assume that additional resources will be forthcoming should decision makers decide to adopt the program proposal.

When resource requirements have been determined, the analyst should then apportion costs into specific categories. The cost work sheet in Exhibit 8.3 shows basic cost items that are typically considered. This includes such things as salaries and wages, personnel costs (i.e., social security, retirement and insurance), materials and supplies, training and overhead costs in support of the program (i.e., payroll preparation, building maintenance, motor pool). Such items tend to be recurring costs in support of operations and maintenance year after year. Investment costs that are necessary to initiate program alternatives in the early stages must also be accounted for. These do not recur from year to year and include such items as land acquisition, facility construction, renovations, new equipment as well as initial planning, development and engineering costs.

Once cost items are accounted for, it is then necessary to estimate future costs. In most cases, the present program extended at its present level should be one of the alternatives costed out. This gives decision makers a base line to use in comparing the other alternatives. The present program is also a good place to begin since it will be the easiest to estimate. As discussed in the previous chapter, cost estimates are usually the most difficult to calculate for those alternatives that diverge substantially from the present program. Exhibit 8.4 presents a list of considerations to guide the analyst in making such calculations.[2] In addition, the following discussion describes various strategies for generating data.[3]

Current cost data applied to the future. This approach is applicable to costs that are not likely to change appreciably. For example, the most recent salary and employee benefit rates could be used to estimate future personnel costs, or current costs of supplies and equipment could be used to estimate operational and maintenance costs. This form of cost projection is burdened by some severe limitations, particularly when costs are likely to rise because of in-

EXHIBIT 8.2. SAMPLE RESOURCE ANALYSIS WORK SHEET. What resources will be needed to implement a program depend on the kinds of activities identified to meet the program objective successfully. This work sheet illustrates the relatedness of activities, required resources, and resource discrepancies.

Objective: *Increase number of volunteers in prevention programs by 33% (8/1/78)*

1. Activities	2. Resources required				3. Resources available				4. Discrepancies	5. Comments
	No. of persons	Skills	Financial	Other materials	No. of persons	Skills	Financial	Other materials		
Media campaign										
1. Gather information	1 for a month	Research	$400 (car mileage, phone)	Photo-copying	Wood-stein available	OK	OK $400	OK	None	
2. Produce TV spots	6 for 3 mos. ea.	Advertising	$18,500	Complete photo editing and production	1 for 3 mos.	No	OK $18,500	No	Skills & equipment for spot production	Subcontract to Wonder Workers, Inc.
3. Distribute spots	1 for 6 weeks	Meeting people, understand media prog.	$325 (mileage)	None	Olson OK	OK	OK $325	OK	None	
										Total cost, this phase, $19,225

SOURCE: Adapted from the National Institute on Drug Abuse, *Prevention Planning Workbook.* Vol. 1, Washington, DC: U.S. Government Printing Office, 1981, p. 48.

flation or where the demand for services change. The need to modify equipment or the availability of new technology will also add to costs.

Price estimates. Where certain types of equipment or facilities are required, sales firms can provide price quotations. Such quotes should be fairly accurate where items are to be used in their existing form or where minor modifications are likely to be required. The analyst, however, should be wary that actual production costs may prove to be higher than initially estimated by vendors.

EXHIBIT 8.3. SAMPLE COST ESTIMATION WORK SHEET. Specific items should be listed under the appropriate category. Different categories can be created to conform to local accounting systems.

   I. Salaries and Wages—salaries and wages for full-time, part-time, and seasonal employees by classification.

  II. Other Personnel Costs
     A. Social Security
     B. Retirement
     C. Medical Insurance
     D. Life Insurance
     E. Recruitment Costs
     F. Training
     G. Workmen's Compensation
     H. Unemployment Insurance
     I. Uniforms and Safety Equipment
     J. Local and Out-of-Town Travel
     K. Other

 III. Operating Materials and Supplies—normal items required to perform the usual functions of the program, i.e., pencils, lumber, spare parts.
     A. Desk-Top Supplies
     B. Postage
     C. Photocopying Supplies
     D. Other

 IV. Equipment
     A. Office Equipment
     B. Vehicles
     C. Large Tools
     D. Computer Hardware
     E. Other

  V. Contractual Services—payments to individuals or firms outside the government for services rendered or payments to other government departments for support services.
     A. Consultants
     B. Maintenance Contracts
     C. Facilities Rental

D. Computer Time
E. Telephone
F. Transportation (Air, Rail, etc.)
G. Utilities
H. Other

VI. Grants and Subsidies—payments directly to citizens (welfare, etc.) or to nongovernment agencies or other jurisdictions for services to citizens.
A. Welfare Payments
B. Community Service Agencies
C. Other Jurisdictions
D. Other

VII. Overhead—costs incurred by other departments in support of this program.
A. Payroll Preparation
B. Accounting
C. Purchasing
D. Interdepartmental Mail
E. Building Maintenance
F. Motor Pool
G. Other

VIII. Capital Expenditures—purchase or construction of major facilities, usually financed differently than other categories.
A. Land Acquisition
B. Facility Construction
C. Equipment for New Facilities
D. Major Renovations
E. Debt Service (interest on bonds sold to finance above)

IX. Increased costs or savings that will be realized in other programs as a result of implementing this alternative.

SOURCE: Public Technology, Inc., *Program Evaluation and Analysis*. Washington, D.C.: U.S. Department of Housing and Urban Development, Nov. 1978, p. 36.

Technical estimates. Technical experts are another useful resource for estimating costs of new program components. Here, an experienced expert dissects the program proposal into as many component parts as may be necessary and cost estimates are made for each part. This, however, can be very time-consuming where many program alternatives are being considered.

Statistical estimation. Whenever possible, statistics should be used to analyze data on past costs and performance as the basis for inferences on future costs and performance. For example, to estimate fuel and maintenance costs of service vehicles, costs for the previous year for all vehicles can be divided by the number of vehicles to produce an average cost per vehicle. This, of course, assumes no price increases or technical changes in the vehicles to be used. The average price per vehicle could then be used to estimate the cost of alternative pro-

EXHIBIT 8.4. ESTIMATING COSTS

Determine which costs are fixed and which costs are variable for each alternative.

For example, if a drug control agency would like to change from one type of outreach operation to another, it is necessary to identify which of the facilities and functional activities already in use can be used in the revised operation. These are fixed costs. Certain supervisory and facility costs may be only partially affected by the change. Only those elements of costs to be increased and decreased in changing from one system of operation to another are variable. (In the long run, however, no costs are fixed. Even the cost of departmental supervision is likely to increase as more programs are added.)

Determine which costs are likely to vary significantly among the alternatives being considered.

For example, if all of the alternatives require the same facilities and impose the same degree of use on existing facilities, then facility and maintenance costs would be the same and the analysis would not have to focus on them. This does not mean that such cost elements can be ignored; merely that the same value for these elements should be used for each applicable alternative.

Determine the marginal or additional costs to be incurred for a specific alternative, not the average costs.

For example, suppose an agency must decide whether to add one more service vehicle or two more service vehicles. The marginal cost of the second is how much more money it costs to buy one. Quantity discounts, for example, might reduce the unit cost for the second vehicle. If one vehicle could be obtained for $10,000 and two for $17,000, the relevant cost of the second is $7,000, not $8,500 which is the average cost.

Though you may wish to determine sunk costs, they are not relevant.

Costs that have already been incurred are not relevant. For example, the fact that an agency invested $20,000 in a computerized data system is not relevant to the cost analysis unless there is a potential salvage value in that system for one or more of the alternatives. Recommending an inferior alternative because of the past expenditure is throwing good money after bad unless there may be political repercussions, e.g., citizens or investors may complain of poor planning and wastefulness.

Determine and include all costs regardless of what organizational unit they are connected with.

Costs are often carried by more than one agency or account. For example, vehicle maintenance is usually performed in the central garage of a municipality. The costs of this maintenance should be included in the costs of programs that use the vehicles. Building maintenance is another example. In addition, employee benefits, which may add 15 to 30 percent to personnel costs, are usually charged to a separate account. Capital costs, even though handled in other funds and in a separate budget document, also must be included in cost estimates.

Determine the future cost implications of each alternative.

For example, a federal, state or private grant usually pays the cost of a new program for the first year or two with the understanding that the agency must assume the full burden after that. The costs of continuing the program beyond the grant period should be estimated. In addition, a decision to build a facility or buy a large item of equipment in one budget year imposes future operating and maintenance costs.

Estimate all revenues that may be produced for each alternative.

Some services charge a fee such as for health services or for the use of recreation facilities. Revenues should be listed either as an offset to total costs or as a side benefit.

Where possible, determine opportunity costs.

If resources are put into one program, opportunities to use the same resources elsewhere are foregone. The value of foregone opportunities is the opportunity cost of putting resources into the selected program. For example, a mental health organization might use land it already owns for a new building. It would, therefore, not incur any additional land costs in this alternative, but would be giving up the opportunity to use the land for other purposes. This would have to be considered when comparing it with other alternatives which will not use the land. This should be separately identified (as a negative benefit) so as not to distort the estimation of funding outlays actually needed for an alternative.

SOURCE: Based on *Public Technology, Inc., Program Evaluation and Analysis.* Washington, D.C.: U.S. Department of Housing and Urban Development, Nov. 1978; pp. 38, 39.

grams using any number of vehicles of the same kind. A more sophisticated statistical technique which can be employed is regression analysis.[4] To illustrate, it can be assumed that the maintenance cost per vehicle will increase as the total mileage of each vehicle increases. Drawing on data from the past year, the analyst can estimate future maintenance costs of similar service vehicles as derived from the regression equation. A statistician with some background in use of the computer can provide the necessary assistance for doing this.

Because of the uncertainty involved, estimating costs poses many difficulties. This is especially the case where unfamiliar alternatives are being analyzed. Where cost estimates cannot be made with a high degree of accuracy, the analyst should indicate this or else the final recommendations may be misleading. Some alternatives, furthermore, are more likely to be affected by future price increases than others and the rate of increase would tend to vary for each cost component—e.g., wages and salaries, facility construction, equipment. If the analyst decides to adjust for price changes, the same adjustments should apply to all alternatives.

Cost estimates should be entered in the appropriate categories of the cost work sheet for each of the years in which the program analysis applies, e.g., over the next three years. After the cost estimation work sheet has been completed, the analyst should prepare for the next step which is the collection of effectiveness data.

STEP 3—COLLECTING EFFECTIVENESS DATA

Just as the costs of program alternatives must be estimated as a criterion for ultimately choosing from among them, so, too, must effectiveness be estimated. Though such calculations are difficult to make, they are a necessary part of program design procedures.[5] Here the analyst must attempt to estimate the future effectiveness of each alternative in accomplishing the purposes of the program. This requires an examination of the goals, objectives and especially the performance criteria that were earlier defined for the program. Performance criteria are the basis for analysing the likely effectiveness of each alternative; or, to state it another way, the analyst must try to predict the effects of each program alternative for each criterion specified. For example, a criterion for a foster care agency may be to increase the number of placements of children with special needs (i.e., minority or handicapped) by 20% over the next year. In estimating effectiveness, the analyst would have to determine what effect each alternative is likely to have on such placements. Some general approaches for estimating effectiveness are described as follows.

Performance data of past programs. Where alternatives represent only minimal variations of existing programs, performance data of past programs can be used to estimate future performance. This assumes that conditions will not change substantially in the future. To illustrate, if placement of minority and handicapped children has been 10% over the past year, this figure can be used to forecast placements for the same program in the immediate future. One problem with this method, however, is that it assumes the availability of performance data. Because many jurisdictions do not collect such information, a special study may be necessary. Another problem with this approach is that it assumes that unadjusted data, where available, are likely to remain stable. This assumption is questionable.

Adjusted performance projections. The basic strategy in this approach is to forecast changing future conditions and then estimate the likely effects of such changes on program performance. In addition to scenario writing, the use of time series data which reveal past trends over a period of years is another technique for projecting the future.[6] For example, if placements of minority and handicapped children show a gradual increase of from 6% to 10% over the past four years, it can be assumed that the rate is likely to continue to increase to approximately 14% over the next four years. Other factors, however, must also be considered. Particularly important are demographic trends in the general population and among clients being served, distinguishing for age, sex, income, race, and location among other characteristics. As previously referred to in Chapter Three, any changes among certain groupings portends new needs and requires, therefore, modifications in the quality or quantity of services provided if the desired effects are to be realized. Changes in the physical features of a neighborhood caused by new housing and transportation will also affect future program performance. Thus, new middle-income single-family housing to be completed during the year in a particular neighborhood will place a heavier demand on school and recreational services and this in turn should impact on estimates of program effectiveness in these service areas.

Experiences of other agencies. Where new alternatives or extensive modifications of old alternatives are being considered, it is a good idea to inquire into the experiences of other agencies that have already tried them. Any kind of evaluative information on how these programs worked would be very useful. Caution should be used where only general reports are available, for they may be public relations rather than a source of valid information. Members of the project team may wish to make on-site visits to observe first hand and to obtain detailed information on program operations. It usually takes six to twelve months and often longer for a new program to stablize. Programs which have been in operation for shorter periods of time should be examined with considerable caution since the full effects, both intended and unintended, will usually not have been determined.

Estimates based on specifications. In some cases, alternatives may be identified that involve new methods or techniques for which data are not available. When this happens, the analyst has to synthesize an estimate from known facts about the alternative or use estimates based on expected characteristics of the proposed operation. For example, the likely effects of a new computerized health data system for the rapid dissemination of health information could be estimated by using information based on the technical specifications of the system. Similar to the other approaches, it is also necessary to estimate whether effectiveness is likely to change in the future given changing conditions.

Use of experts. Where it is not possible to use the methods referred to above, the analyst may resort to expert judgement. Experts are persons who have substantial experience in particular program areas. As such, they can be called upon to make short-run and/or long-run estimates of the effectiveness of proposed alternatives or they can identify factors which are necessary for the estimation of effectiveness. Expert judgements should be derived through systematic procedures and should not be confused with offhand opinion. Furthermore, they should be documented with supporting justification wherever possible. To illustrate, experts could rank alternatives as based on a particular criterion, e.g., whether a proposed reading program is likely to improve reading scores (+), lower reading scores (—), or have no effect (0).

Mock debate. In this approach, each alternative is assigned to a team which then builds a case for and against it. This method is especially useful where a program will have varying impacts on different groups being serviced. For example, a neighborhood health and recreation program will affect particular age groups differently and may even contribute negative effects in some instances: elderly persons may be made vulnerable to muggers if the program is offered in an isolated area at night; low-income children may be excluded if working parents cannot take them to the facility. An adversary process can thereby provide the project team with a broader perspective of the pros and cons of each alternative.

Testing. Situations arise where it is not possible to make reasonably accurate estimates of program effects. If an agency believes that a certain alternative is of substantial merit, but is uncertain about how it will impact on clients or other groups being served, it could be implemented on a trial basis. This strategy is appropriate where the program is of limited scale and does not require heavy initial investments. This can be illustrated in the case of an "experimental" family education program that attempts to motivate low-income minority mothers by exposing them to speakers of similar backgrounds who have dealt successfully with certain problems. A mental health board may decide to introduce the program on a one-year basis in one or two neighborhood centers in order to obtain information on the effectiveness of such a strategy. There are some problems with this approach, however. Start-up difficulties might impede a realistic assessment of how the program would perform under more normal circumstances. In addition, the so-called "Hawthorne" effect could interfere. This refers to the possibility that special treatment accorded clients during the trial period could skew performance indicators leading to invalid conclusions.

STEP 4—COLLECTING FEASIBILITY INFORMATION

An aspect of program design that is often ignored pertains to the feasibility of implementing alternatives. Such form of omission is unfortunate for it cannot be assumed that each alternative will have the same chance of success in the agency environment. Some alternatives will pose more difficulties than others, and this should be accounted for in advance so as to avoid obstacles which could delay or permanently block them. As discussed previously in the context of organizational change, feasibility assessment focuses on the following concerns: What are the major barriers to implementation? What characteristics make a particular alternative especially attractive in facilitating implementation?[7]

Exhibit 8.5 is intended to serve as a guide to help the analyst identify those specific factors which bear directly on implementation. The questions posed here should be reviewed by agency heads and other participating officials who have had experience with political issues. Pertinent factors should then be described in sufficient detail for each alternative. Having done this, alternatives may be reconsidered in light of either special problems or special opportunities in the implementation process. In some cases, modifications may be necessary to overcome problems or to better facilitate proposed changes. Where this happens, the analyst should reexamine the impact of any modification on the cost and effectiveness estimates that were previously made. In doing the narrative report, the analyst may also wish to rank alternatives as to which one is 'most feasible', 'moderately feasible', or 'least feasible'.

EXHIBIT 8.5. ESTIMATING FEASIBILITY. The following questions must be weighed to estimate the feasibility of implementing program alternatives.

How many agencies and organizations must cooperate or participate in order to insure successful implementation?

The more people and groups required to provide approval or support for an alternative, the more difficult implementation is likely to be.

Are there client groups whose interests will be directly affected by a change in existing services?
Alternatives that increase or maintain the level of services will present fewer implementation difficulties than those that reduce the level of services.

To what extent does the alternative threaten jobs?
Where jobs are threatened, opposition can be substantial, especially where a strong employee's organization is present.

To what extent are special personnel capabilities required?
Implementation will be difficult where personnel with the required skills are not available. In addition, special training may be necessary.

To what extent does the alternative require changes in the routines of employees?
Employees may be unable or unwilling to conform to the routines of the alternative. For example, it may require different working hours or location of employees which may lead to resistance.

Are the sources of funds and their availability fairly certain?
Some sources of funds may be more reliable than others. Alternatives requiring special funding support may be subject to uncertainty, particularly during periods of retrenchment.

Are there complex legal questions?
The more complex the legal aspects of implementing an alternative are, the greater the likelihood for delay; all the more so where new legislation is required.

To what extent is public opinion for or against the alternative?
If public discussion has polarized the community, decision makers may find the alternative unattractive where implementation will alienate one faction or another.

To what extent does the alternative require space or facilities that may be difficult to obtain?
For example, neighborhood populations may resist the location of drug treatment centers, mental health facilities, nursing homes, halfway houses, etc., in their neighborhoods.

To what extent does the alternative involve technological uncertainties?
Operational difficulties that result from new technologies may increase costs, reduce effectiveness, and delay and even prevent implementation.

Has a recent crisis generated support for the alternative?
Implementation problems could be overcome if the problem is clearly recognized by the community. For example, a recent wave of drug abuse cases among local juveniles may greatly improve the chances of gaining acceptance for a local treatment center.

How sensitive is the alternative to timing?
Implementation of program alternatives can be delayed for long periods of time. Such delays can invalidate costs and effectiveness estimates or impede coordination with a related program. Another common timing problem is underestimating lead time necessary for program initiation. If the alternative requires recruitment and/or training of key personnel, delays can be very difficult to estimate. The longer the lead time required, the longer the delay before potential benefits are realized.

SOURCE: Adapted from Public Technology, Inc., *Program Evaluation and Analysis.* Washington, D.C.: U.S. Department of Housing and Urban Development, Nov. 1978, p. 41.

SUMMARY

Successful problem solving requires finding the best possible solution. Thus, it is necessary to estimate and compare such factors as service demand, costs, and effectiveness for each alternative. How to identify and collect such data has been the basic interest of this chapter. From the perspective of organization change, moreover, the analyst must also estimate the feasibility of implementing alternatives in the agency environment. Indeed, some cost-effective alternatives may not be very feasible. The greater the effort made in assembling all the necessary information, the stronger the foundation on which to choose among alternatives.

NOTES

1. On estimating service demand, see, also, Rossi, Peter H., and Freeman, Howard E., *Evaluation, A Systematic Approach* (Beverly Hills, Cal.: Sage Publications, 2nd Edition, 1982), Chap. 3.

2. A useful discussion of cost-estimating is to be found in Durham, T.R., *An Introduction to Benefit-Cost Analysis for Evaluating Public Programs* (Croton-on-Hudson, N.Y.: Policy Studies Associates, 1977).

3. The discussion on estimating costs is based largely on Public Technology, Inc., *Program Evaluation and Analysis*, pp. 35–39; and Hatry, Harry, *Program Analysis for State and Local Governments*, pp. 57–71.

4. For a thorough and readable treatment of regression analysis see Kerlinger, Fred N., and Pedhazur, Elazar J., *Multiple Regression in Behavior Research* (New York: Holt, Rinehard and Winston, 1973).

5. See Hatry, Harry, *Program Analysis for State and Local Governments*, Chap. 5; and Public Technology, Inc., *Program Evaluation and Analysis*, pp. 37–40.

6. See Box, G.E.P., and Jenkins, G.M., *Time Series Analysis: Forecasting and Control* (San Francisco: Holden-Day, 1969); and Wheelwright, S.C., and Makridis, S., *Forecasting Methods for Management* (New York: John Wiley, 1973).

7. A useful approach for gauging political factors is presented in Coplin, William D., and O'Leary, Michael K., *Everyman's Prince*. See, also, Hatry, Harry, *Program Analysis for State and Local Governments*, Chap. 7.

CHAPTER 9

SYNTHESIZING THE DATA _____

After the data on service demand, costs, effectiveness and feasibility have been collected, the analyst must combine all this information to be able to compare alternatives and draw conclusions. In this way, the analyst can provide decision makers with a limited number of the best possible alternatives along with supporting information on which they can base a decision. While the analyst and the project team should weigh the relative merits of alternatives in developing conclusions as part of a final report, they are not expected to provide the answer to the problem; that is the responsibility of the decision makers.

STEP 1—ORGANIZING THE DATA

The first step in synthesizing the data is to consolidate and organize all of the available data that has been collected for each alternative. Data should include: (1) a description of each alternative specifying procedures and activities and the organizational units to be involved; (2) estimates of service demand; (3) a cost estimation work sheet; (4) a work sheet summarizing effectiveness estimates; and (5) a work sheet summarizing implementation feasibility. After the data have been compiled for all of the alternatives, the analyst should then prepare to make comparisons.

STEP 2—COMPARING THE DATA

Here the analyst compares the relative costs of the alternatives, the relative effectiveness, and the respective feasibility summaries. It is recommended that the data be presented in tables wherever possible to assist the decision makers who usually require quick and easy access to the available information. This is illustrated in Exhibit 9.1 which presents cost data for four proposed alternatives over a two year period. Viewing this, decision makers can quickly determine which alternatives have high capital costs, which ones have high personnel costs, and which ones show high costs for contract services. Public officials usually have a special interest in personnel costs since they are recurring in most service areas and are difficult to contain.

Effectiveness data and cost totals for three of the proposed alternatives are presented in Exhibit 9.2. They provide a more detailed basis for judging the pros and cons of revisions being considered for a manpower development and training program. The intended purpose of this project is to improve the work capabilities of the hard core unemployed among inner-city minority persons. Specific objectives are to (1) increase the number of welfare dependent persons receiving training; (2) induce positive attitudes toward work among the trainees; and (3) increase the number of job placements within six months of completing training. Analysis was based on the assumption that the number of trainees in future years would remain at about 650 per year. Estimates of effectiveness appear to favor Alternative I though costs would tend to be somewhat higher than the others over two years. It should be noted, however, that effectiveness measures as presented here are not comprehensive. The quality of training to be given is ignored and long-term effects are not examined. Nevertheless, the data do provide some useful basis for comparison.

Feasibility factors can be listed separately under 'advantages' or 'disadvantages.' For example, a particular alternative would be disadvantaged where it is discerned that welfare workers have little or no interest in certain types of training; or where labor unions indicate opposition to an increase in available manpower that will result from training.

EXHIBIT 9.1. COST COMPARISONS. This table shows a cost comparison of four program alternatives by cost category. Such a table would allow decision makers to determine which alternatives would be more labor-intensive or capital expenditures intensive. The personnel category includes salaries, fringe benefits, and personnel-related costs such as uniforms and training expenses.

Alternative	#1	#2	#3	#4
First Year				
Personnel	$ 80,000	$ 75,000	$ 50,000	$30,000
Capital Equipment	$ 10,000	$ 15,000	$ 10,000	$ 10,000
Contract Services	—	—	$ 10,000	$ 40,000
Other Expenditures	$ 3,000	$ 4,000	$ 4,000	$ 5,000
Total	$ 93,000	$ 94,000	$ 74,000	$ 85,000
Second Year				
Personnel	$ 75,000	$ 65,000	$ 40,000	$ 20,000
Capital Equipment	—	—	$ 2,000	—
Contract Services	—	—	—	$ 40,000
Other Expenditures	$ 2,000	$ 2,000	$ 3,000	$ 3,000
Total	$ 77,000	$ 67,000	$ 45,000	$ 63,000
GRAND TOTAL	$170,000	$161,000	$119.000	$148,000

EXHIBIT 9.2. EFFECTIVENESS AND COSTS OF MANPOWER TRAINING ALTERNATIVES. This table shows a comparison of three program alternatives using criteria of likely effectiveness and costs.

Criteria	Alternative I		Alternative II		Alternative III	
	First Year[a]	Second Year	First Year[a]	Second Year	First Year[a]	Second Year
1. Number welfare-dependent trainees	100-200	190-300	Same as Alternative I		100-130	120-200
2. Number showing positive work orientation	300-400	500-600	Same as Alternative I		250-350	400-500
3. Number of job placements	300	400	250	300	200	300
4. Reduction in welfare dependencies of family units	80-150	100-200	80-120	100-200	80-100	100-150
Costs ($000)— Federal, state, and local	93	77	94	67	74	45

[a]Based on six months program development time and only six months operating time.

STEP 3—DRAWING CONCLUSIONS

Viewing Exhibit 9.2, some persons may be prepared to argue that Alternative II is more cost effective than the other two. This, however, assumes that each criterion carries equal weight. Given their special stakes and interests, decision makers may attach more importance to certain criteria and less importance to others. Furthermore, an alternative may give promise of certain intangible benefits that cannot be measured. These could include such factors as greater control in the administrative process, catering to the needs of important constituencies, reducing citizen complaints, or enhancing the political appeal of elected officials.

In presenting conclusions, the analyst should identify one or two alternatives that appear to have relative merit on the basis of the full range of information that has been collected. As previously mentioned, however, the final decision as to which alternative should be adopted rests with top management and officials.

SUMMARY

The process of selecting the most appropriate solution to any given problem is very much at the heart of the program design process. This requires not only the collection of information about how each alternative is likely to function, but, as this chapter shows, comparing the likely costs and benefits of each alternative through the careful organization of all pertinent data. The decision to select an alternative, however, rests with top management and officials. Preparation of a report to facilitate this choice is covered in the next chapter.

CHAPTER 10

COMMUNICATING THE RESULTS

Program design as described in the previous chapters is a painstaking endeavor. It is based largely on the rational problem-solver model which involves defining the problem, defining or redefining goals and objectives in light of the problem, establishing performance criteria, generating program alternatives, and estimating costs, effectiveness and feasibility. Yet, all of this is likely to be wasted effort if the findings are not presented in a way which is understandable and useful to the decision makers and administrators who must act on them. Top managers, officials and staff must be sold on the proposal so that their support can be counted on for adoption and subsequent implementation.

Using strategies of organizational change, the project team must be able to package and communicate the program that it has designed. Preliminary to any formal presentation, informal discussion through personal contacts will usually help to sensitize decision makers to the proposal. Especially important is the writing and presentation of the final report which should explain the proposed program lucidly and convincingly. This is the focus of the present chapter.

Three basic steps are described for communicating the results of the program design project: (1) preparation of a draft report; (2) review of the draft report by concerned parties; and (3) transmission of the final report to officials.

STEP 1—PREPARING THE DRAFT REPORT

A necessary consideration in preparing the draft report is that it be written with its special audiences in mind. Usually more than one audience is involved. One kind of audience consists of ranking officials such as legislators, the chief administrative officer and key staff, department heads who may be affected, and community leaders. Such persons have many demands on their time and are likely to want a summary report with recommendations for their consideration. A second kind of audience is the agency administrators who will be responsible for administering the program that has been designed and who are likely to have some specific concerns about operations and organization. This group will be interested in how the project team arrived at their recommendations and conclusions and whether the report is fully justified from the criteria of cost-effectiveness and feasibility. Sometimes there is a third audience consisting of analytical personnel from other agencies or jurisdictions who would like to review the data and techniques used to generate that data.[1]

The report outline in Exhibit 10.1 addresses this by prescribing two or three small reports for each audience: an executive summary for officials and legislators; a management report for middle-level administrators and project leaders who are to be responsible for carrying-out the program; and a technical report for analytical personnel. This format provides some greater assurance that the report will meet the interests and needs of the readers. The outline can also be used to prepare one consolidated report if the project team decides that this is what is appropriate. Where separate reports are to be submitted, the problem statement and program description in Section I of the outline should precede the management report in Section II; and, where this is called for, the technical report in Section III should also be included. For additional illustration, a final report in completed form is presented in Appendix D.

EXHIBIT 10.1. REPORT OUTLINE. Below is a suggested outline for a program design report. The outline lends itself to preparing one consolidated report, or two or three separate smaller reports for various target audiences.

I. Executive Summary—of primary interest to elected officials, legislators, chief executive officers, and administrators. Approximately 2-4 pages.
    A. Introduction
        1. What is this document and why has it been written? For whom has it been written?
        2. What does this document contain?
    B. Problem Statement—a brief statement of the problem or needs addressed by the program.
        1. What is the problem or need(s) that the program is intended to deal with? Identify indicators that a problem/need exists.
        2. What are the causes of the problem or need(s)?
        3. What are the impacts of the problem on the community? How significant are the impacts? Is there a geographic or demographic focus?
    C. Program Description
        1. What are the program goals and objectives being addressed? (Must be defined anew for a new program.)
        2. How does the present program attempt to alleviate the problem outlined above? (Where a program does not presently exist, describe any present efforts to deal with the problem.)

---

3. What are the positive accomplishments and apparent shortcomings of the program? (Where a program does not exist, this is an obvious shortcoming.)

D. Methodology—brief description of how the study was conducted.

E. Recommendations and Conclusions—summarize the one or two alternatives that the analyst believes show the greatest promise. List those major action items necessary to implement the various alternatives and estimate the implementation time frame.

II. Management Report—a 10 to 20 page report written for chief executives or assistants, department or division administrators, and task force or project leaders who are responsible for the program.

A. Methodology
   1. Reiterate program goals and objectives. Specify performance criteria.
   2. Describe all of the alternatives considered in the analysis. How would each alternative work? What organizational units would be involved? What procedures must be developed? What resource will be required? Include a summary of advantages and disadvantages for each and an indication of the final disposition of each stated as a final recommendation—e.g., rejected as infeasible, dropped for lack of information, considered a secondary alternative, etc.
   3. Describe approaches used to estimate costs, effectiveness, and implementation feasibility.
   4. Present data summaries on costs and effectiveness in tabular or graph form.

B. Recommendations and Conclusions—list each recommendation and conclusion and discussion of the rationale behind it. If the list is extensive, the analyst should highlight only the more important items.

C. Implementation—discuss considerations concerning the implementation of recommendations. The nature of implementation activities, of course, will depend upon management decisions made in response to the study. The possible make-up of an implementation team should be discussed, and the need for a significant role for the analyst during implementation should be stressed.
   1. Present implementation workplan. (See Chapter Eleven.)
   2. List criteria for measuring progress. (See Chapter Eleven.)
   3. List data collection methods. (See Chapter Eleven.)

III. Technical Report—written for analytical personnel from other agencies or jurisdictions.

A. Data—raw data collected and technical notes documenting assumptions used in making calculations.

B. Data Sources—documentation on where various data items were obtained.

C. Methodology (optional)—documentation of all calculations used in projections, estimations, evaluation criteria measurements.

STEP 2—REVIEWING THE DRAFT REPORT

Good writing and clarity of explanation is necessary if the proposed program is to be given proper consideration by responsible officials. The analyst must be wary of misinterpretation of statements in the report as a hazard to be avoided at all costs.[2] For these reasons, several readings of the draft report are a necessary precautionary measure before it is submitted in final form. During the first reading, other members of the project team and particularly the team leader should review the report to make sure that all necessary material has been included and that there are no misleading statements. For the second reading, the report should be reviewed by another analyst to check on methodology and validity. For the third reading, someone who has not been involved in the study should review it to determine if the language is understandable and clear of jargon. If someone with editorial experience is available, a critique should also be made of grammar and style.[3] Finally, and perhaps most important, the draft report should be reviewed by agency personnel who are likely to be involved and by community groups that are likely to be affected. Where it is considered to be appropriate, representatives from personnel associations or unions should be allowed a reading since their cooperation may be required.

Three or four weeks should be allowed for this review process to take place. The analyst should proceed in a systematic manner by first making a list of persons or groups who are expected to play a role. To assist the reviewers, a list of questions could be provided for their guidance. While the questions should vary depending on the nature of the project, some general questions that might ordinarily be included are presented in Exercise 10.1. The list of questions and a final date for returning comments should accompany the draft report sent to each reviewer. If the reader is not presently engaged in a program design project, he or she should complete this exercise by reviewing an available report in an agency of interest.

Comments that are returned should come under the purview of the team leader who decides which ones justify changes in the report. Another strategy is to include comments in an appendix. The project team may also decide to respond to these comments in writing if they decide that this would be useful. In this way, the final report can keep its integrity without losing credibility with officials.

STEP 3—TRANSMITTING THE FINAL REPORT

After the reviews have been studied by the project team and comments incorporated into the report, it is ready to be submitted in final form to the decision makers. Specific procedures for doing this will vary with local protocol. In most situations, an oral presentation is desirable after the decision makers have had time to read the written report. An oral presentation allows the project team to highlight those aspects of the program design they think are important. In addition, it gives the decision makers a chance to ask questions and clear up any confusion they may have.

The team leader should consult with top management as to specific topics to be addressed and the mode of delivery. While other members of the team could participate in the presentation, particularly as a way of giving them recognition for their work, the leader

EXERCISE 10.1. REVIEWING THE REPORT. Where answers to the questions posed below are negative, provide elaboration to the problems that have been noted.

Is the organization of the report sound?

Is the report written clearly and is it understandable?

Have any important issues been overlooked?

Does the report contain irrelevant material?

Are there any statements that could be considered unfair or misleading?

Does the report adequately document and support the conclusions and recommendations?

Are there any factual errors?

Does the report provide enough information to support a decision about the program?

Does the report respond to basic issues, questions, or problems?

Where are the organizational, political or legal pitfalls?

should be wary of a disjointed 'show and tell' approach that lacks consistency. It may therefore be advisable to allow the analyst to coordinate the overall presentation including the preparation of visual aids.

Overall, both the report and the oral presentation should encourage officials to follow-up through a course of action and a commitment of resources. Unless this is done, with some immediate steps specified, the program proposal is not likely to be realized.

SUMMARY

This chapter has focused on the importance of effectively communicating the results of the program design project to decision makers. This involves both informal discussion preliminary to a formal report and then packaging the report so that it is presented under the best possible circumstances. In doing this, the analyst must be aware of who it is that he or she is trying to communicate to and what their particular interests are. In drafting the report, the analyst should involve as many concerned parties as possible in the review process. The more thorough the review, the greater the likelihood that errors and misunderstandings can be avoided. Ultimately, a well-written report that is carefully presented according to local protocol should encourage decision makers to adopt and implement the proposal.

NOTES

1. Methods of communicating to different audiences in an organizational setting are analyzed in Rogers, Everett M., and Agarwala-Rogers, Rahka *Communication in Organizations* (New York: The Free Press, 1976).

2. Problems of communicating in bureaucracies are discussed by Downs, Anthony, *Inside-Bureaucracy* (Boston: Little, Brown & Company, 1967), pp. 116–118; also Wilensky, Harold L., *Organizational Intelligence: Knowledge and Policy in Government and Industry* (New York: Basic Books, 1967), pp. 41–74.

3. For guidance on style in the writing of a report, see Strunk, Jr., William, and White, E. B., *The Elements of Style* (New York: Macmillan, 1959); and Fowler, H. W., *A Dictionary of Modern English Usage* (New York: Oxford University Press, 1965).

CHAPTER 11

PREPARING FOR IMPLEMENTATION

Members of the project team should be wary of getting so involved in the program design project that they see it as the final product; if the project is not implemented, nothing will have been achieved in the way of improved public service. The project report is one crucial step to be followed by still other steps that deal with the complex task of program implementation. This requires preparation and planning for implementation as based on the findings of the project report. Four basic steps are involved: (1) forming an implementation team; (2) preparing an implementation workplan; (3) selecting methods for monitoring implementation progress; and (4) follow-up strategies.

STEP 1—FORMING AN IMPLEMENTATION TEAM

Just as a project team must be established to design a program and recommend alternatives, an implementation team must be established to begin detailed planning for carrying out those alternatives. This assumes that the decision makers have made the decision to adopt one or more alternatives that have been proposed. To assure continuity and to capitalize on experience gained during the program phase, it is recommended that the project leader for the implementation team should be the same person who was responsible for the previous program design project. Others to be selected should include personnel from the program agencies who have knowledge of the program area and the analyst who has special knowledge of the program design project. The analyst should be responsible for monitoring the progress of implementation. In some instances, representatives from outside groups such as labor and community organizations should be included if they are important to the implementation process. To better assure cooperation, a lead role should be given to an appropriate individual from the agency most directly involved in implementation.

STEP 2—PREPARING AN IMPLEMENTATION WORKPLAN

Following the formation of an implementation team, a workplan covering implementation tasks should be prepared to serve as a guide for all those directly involved. In addition to a description of each task, the workplan should include a chart showing the timing and duration of each task and estimates by task of the personnel, resources to be required. An example of a scheduling chart for the implementation of a comprehensive addictive services program is presented in Exhibit 11.1. Here, each major recommendation is listed as a major task with steps necessary to implement the recommendation shown as subtasks. As illustrated in Exhibit 11.2, some jurisdictions attach the name of the individual responsible for carrying out the task by a specified date. In this way, top management is able to know who may be held responsible if the job doesn't get done. In addition, a workplan provides team members with a clear view of where they are going and how they are to get there.

STEP 3—METHODS FOR MONITORING IMPLEMENTATION PROGRESS

Once implementation begins, the team should be prepared to monitor how the program is progressing. The basic concerns in this step are to track changes in the implementation of the program, maintain a record of the program's development, and provide feedback to the program staff on impediments as the program is being installed. Here, the workplan serves as a basic tool with which to determine whether tasks are proceeding according to schedule. But in addition to scheduling, operations, resources, and organizational and political factors must be accounted for. For each of these, appropriate criteria should be defined in advance and incorporated into the implementation workplan.[1]

EXHIBIT 11.1. SCHEDULE FOR THE IMPLEMENTATION OF A COMPREHENSIVE ADDICTIVE SERVICES PROGRAM

TASKS	9/2	9/16	9/30	10/14	10/28	11/11	11/25
1. Collaboration with alcoholism medical board							
a. Designate liaison committee	——						
b. Organizational meeting		——					
c. Meeting on resources		———					
2. Client screening							
a. Staff training		————					
b. Design client eligibility procedures			————				
c. Client selection				—————			
d. Orientation					——		
3. Outreach unit							
a. Field investigators oriented				————			
b. Procedural manual						——	
c. Neighborhood facilities designated							————

EXHIBIT 11.2. ACTION PLAN FOR THE IMPLEMENTATION OF A COMMUNITY-BASED HEALTH EDUCATION PROGRAM

TASK	TARGET DATE	PERSON RESPONSIBLE
1. Establish liaison with community groups		
a. Civic organizations	8/1	J. Jones
b. Neighborhood organizations	8/10	J. Jones
c. School organizations	8/21	S. Badis
2. Development of education materials		
a. Overheads	8/22	L. Bell
b. Education manuals	8/22	R. Meier
3. Conducting workshops		
a. Workshop A	9/15	J. Jones
b. Workshop B	9/20	J. Jones
c. Workshop C	9/25	S. Badis
4. Assessment and written report	10/25	R. Meier

In monitoring *operations,* it is necessary to determine whether different program components are in place and actually functioning as anticipated in the program design. Are citizens or clients actually receiving the service with what effects? Generally, the more discrete functions there are, and the more complex they are, the more difficult it is to coordinate them.[2] In light of this, what evidence is there of distortions or irregularities involving services to citizens or clients? To what extent is measurement providing feedback to strengthen program control? Are any critical elements uncontrollable? In addition, when a program includes more than one site, program implementation among sites should be compared. Between-site differences may provide clues as to why the project may be more implementable in some sites than in others.

On questions of *resources,* it must be determined whether funds for program activities are being distributed according to plan and whether they are sufficient. Are facilities adequate? Are personnel with the appropriate skills and qualities moving into place and are they capable of carrying out their duties as expected? Are supplies and technical equipment available and useable? Where new technology is being introduced, how well is it working?

Perhaps the toughest challenge in program implementation is managing *organizational and political factors.* Program personnel usually have to share authority and retain the support of relevant bureaucratic and political actors while assembling the necessary resources and managing the program. Some programs can be implemented with a minimum involvement of other participants, while others require the active involvement of many participants. In situations which reflect the latter, the team leader and analyst must assess what effects they are having on the program.

Depending on the nature of the program being implemented, the following bureaucratic and political actors that were previously discussed in Chapter Four should be accounted for again: (1) the overhead agencies, (2) other line agencies, (3) elected officials in the same government, (4) higher levels of government, (5) private-sector providers, (6) special interest and community groups, and (7) the media (press and TV). Most of these are beyond the implementation team's direct control, but as previously noted, each of them can affect implementation of the program in one or more of the following ways: by providing or withholding necessary clearances and authorizations; by participating positively or negatively in the actual operations and management of the program; and by producing political support for, or attacks on, the program. Feedback on such matters can be critical to the success of any program. The analyst should attempt to assess the full range of implementation factors at strategic points in time as shown in Exercise 11.1. In the meanwhile, the reader should assess the implementation of a program that he or she is familiar with and that is presently operating as a way of gaining sensitivity.

In addition to the scoring system shown in this exercise, objective data should be collected in assessing implementation. Methods of data collection will vary depending on the time and resources available for monitoring and depending, also, on expectations of accuracy and credibility from the standpoint of who will be using the data. Wherever possible, more than one method to generate measures should be used. Four very useful methods of collecting data are as follows:[3]

EXERCISE 11.1. MONITORING IMPLEMENTATION

How are the following factors affecting implementation? Score plus (+) where the factor is supportive, minus (−) where it poses constraints, or zero (0) where it is not relevant.

	T^1	T^2	T^3	T^4
A. Operational Factors				
1. People being served				
(a) Number of client/citizen transactions				
(b) Reaching clients/citizens				
(c) Effects on clients/citizens				
2. Nature of services				
(a) Number of discrete functions				
(b) Complexity of discrete functions				
(c) Coordination among functions				
3. Evidence of distortions or irregularities				
(a) Involving clients/citizens				
(b) Involving services				
4. Controllability of program				
(a) Measuring program elements				
(b) Uncontrollable critical elements				
B. Nature and Availability of Resources				
1. Money				
(a) Flexibility				
(b) Obtaining additional funding				

2. Personnel T^1 T^2 T^3 T^4
   (a) Qualifications of personnel in place
   (b) Numbers, kinds and quality needed
   (c) Availability of personnel in market
   (d) Attractiveness of program to
       personnel
3. Space
   (a) Adequacy of current facilities
   (b) Availability of facilities
   (c) Special problems in acquiring
       or using space
4. Supplies and technical equipment
   (a) Availability and usability
   (b) New technology

C. Organizational and Political Factors
   1. Overhead agencies
      (a) Number of transactions
      (b) Extent of favorable response
   2. Other line agencies
      (a) Extent of involvement
      (b) Ability to pinpoint responsibility
      (c) Extent of harmonious working
          relations
   3. Elected officials
      (a) Capacity to help or hurt
      (b) Inclination to help or hurt
   4. Higher levels of government
      (a) Extent of authority
      (b) Number of transactions
      (c) Nature of politics
      (d) Extent of favorable response
   5. Private-sector providers
      (a) Availability
      (b) Political problems
      (c) Extent of favorable response
   6. Special-interest groups
      (a) Number and strength
      (b) Inclination to help or hurt
   7. The media (press, TV)
      (a) Level of visibility
      (b) Controversial dimensions
      (c) Extent of favorable response

SOURCE: Based on Gordon Chase, "Implementing a Human Services Program: How Hard Will It Be?" *Public Policy*, Vol. 27, No, 4, Fall 1979, pp. 422, 423.

Examination of records. In a program where records are kept, it may be possible to screen out data which reveal what activities have occurred, what materials and facilities were used, and how, and with whom certain activities took place. The advantage of this method is that it provides evidence of program events as they occurred rather than as events to be reconstructed later. If it appears that the existing records are inadequate, it may be possible to set up a system of keeping records for the purpose of monitoring implementation. Some examples of records which lend themselves to monitoring are attendance and enrollment reports, ledgers, sign-in sheets, minutes, equipment check-outs, personnel files, logs, and assignment cards.

Conduct observations. Here, one or more observers are assigned the responsibility of making regular visits to program sites to record their observations. This can be done in an open-ended manner where an accounting is made of events within a prescribed time frame, or it can be done according to detailed guidelines about what to observe, when and how long to observe, and the method of recording the data, e.g., a questionnaire or a tally sheet. Though observation requires a great deal of time and effort, it is a very useful method because it allows the program to be viewed as it occurs. The observer is obligated, however, to demonstrate that the data collected is reliable by showing that it is consistent across different observers and over time. Another concern in the use of observational methods is that they are not very feasible where the presence of an observer is obtrusive. In some cases it may be necessary for observers to become, at least temporarily, program participants.

Self-report measures. Program personnel are another source of information on how a program is being implemented. Such persons can either be interviewed or can be asked to respond to a questionnaire. Since this can be quite costly if all personnel involved in a program are interviewed, the project team may find it advisable to derive information from a sample of persons performing different tasks. The self-report method, however, has a credibility problem since self-reporting on a person's own behavior may lack objectivity; program personnel may have a self-interest in making the program look good. To control for this, self-reporting information should be obtained from different participants and across different sites and compared for consistency. This approach is probably best used as a secondary source to verify data from other sources.

Client/citizen feedback. The receivers of a service should also be a source of information in monitoring implementation. Client/citizen feedback is useful for the following reasons: service providers may not be aware of what is important to clients; a sense of satisfaction with the service being delivered may not be known; it may be the only way to determine what is actually being delivered; and compared to program staff the clients may have a different understanding of what is being delivered. Client feedback data can be generated through random surveys of clients during different phases of implementation.

STEP 4—FOLLOW-UP STRATEGIES

A remaining question is what can the implementation team do where problems of implementation are detected. One strategy is to let the program continue to operate as is and to settle for whatever results. This is probably what happens in most cases. However, some follow-up strategies should be considered. At the least, the project team should try to show

how specific constraints are likely to influence the costs and effectiveness of the program being implemented. This could lead to a respecification of the program design. Second, the project team might try to suggest variations of the program that could ease implementation. Sometimes this can be done by reducing the number of actors who must provide clearance. For example, by contracting out for part or all of the program, the overhead agencies and restrictive civil service rules can often be avoided. Third, the implementation team could alert program staff about key players who are not cooperating. Strategies could be suggested to encourage cooperation. Sometimes this can be accomplished easily enough through informal meetings or by improving communication. We should note, however, that implementation usually takes place in a public context and candid information on poor performance could provoke hostility among certain participants. Thus, implementation monitoring and feedback must be carried out with a great deal of sensitivity to the participants.

Successful program design and implementation is more of an art than a science. It is a creative process which relies on individuals' abilities and desires to innovate and to change the way organizations function. This can only happen, however, where the needs and interests of officials, practitioners, clients and various political actors that have a stake in the program are carefully managed to preclude conflict and obstruction.

SUMMARY AND CONCLUSIONS

Just as there is the need to plan for a program before it is adopted, this chapter has emphasized the need to plan for a program after it has been adopted. The project team's responsibility, therefore, should not end with the presentation of a report. Members of the team should participate with agency personnel in the implementation of a program after it is adopted; for in public services, a majority of good ideas, however appealing they seem at first glance, are never fully implemented. This means they must treat new program activity differently from existing activity with respect to operations, resources, and organizational and political controls. Monitoring the implementation stage confirms whether the program change is right for the agency as well as for the clients or citizens being served.

Once it is underway, the implementation team must recognize that returns from a new or revised program are different from returns generated by ongoing programs. At the beginning, new programs usually generate more costs than benefits; but, then, returns should increase substantially. Where this is not likely to happen, the program is probably not worth continuing for the risks are too great to justify a lower return. To determine this, program managers should continue to monitor performance. They should ask: "What results should be expected by what date?" When results do not show as expected, they should be able to identify the organizational bottlenecks and make corrections. When a program fails to meet the targets two or three times in a row, program managers do not say: "Let's redouble our efforts." They say: "It's time we did something else."

Perhaps most important of all, the agency should be prepared to abandon that which is no longer productive. Managers should recognize that all forms of service delivery become obsolete sooner or later; and it is better to abandon obsolete services sooner rather than later.

The productive agency reconsiders what it is doing every three or four years and puts on trial every product, process, and technology. Organized abandonment of the obsolete is the one sure way for an organization to focus the vision and energies of its personnel on performance.

Viewing the 1980s, demands for change and innovation in public services are likely to be greater than ever before. To meet the challenge, agencies will need to muster resources; but what will be required above all, as we've tried to show, are innovative attitudes, policies and practices of organizations.

NOTES

1. This is demonstrated by Chase, Gordon, "Implementing a Human Services Program: How Hard Will It Be?" *Public Policy*, Vol: 27, No. 4 (Fall 1979), pp. 385–435.

2. See, for example, Pressman, Jeffrey, and Wildavsky, Aaron, *Implementation* (Berkeley: University of California Press, 1973).

3. See, also, Morris, Lynn Lyons and Fitz-Gibbon, Carol Taylor, *How to Measure Program Implementation* (Beverly Hills, CA: Sage Publications, Inc., 1978).

APPENDIX A: GUIDE TO INFORMATION SOURCES IN PUBLIC SERVICES

Academy for State and Local
  Government
400 North Capital Street
Suite 390
Washington, DC 20001

Airport Operators Council,
  International, Inc.
1700 K Street, NW
Suite 602
Washington, DC 20006

American Association of Port
  Authorities
1612 K Street, NW
Suite 900
Washington, DC 20006

American Association of School
  Administrators
1801 North Moore Street
Arlington, VA 22209

American Association of State
  Highway and Transportation
  Officials
444 North Capital Street
Suite 225
Washington, DC 20001

American Planning Association
American Institute of Certified
  Planners
1776 Massachusetts Avenue, NW
Washington, DC 20036

American Public Health Association
1015 15th Street, NY
3rd Floor
Washington, DC 20005

American Public Power Association
2301 M Street, NW
3rd Floor
Washington, DC 20037

American Public Transit
  Association
1225 Connecticut Avenue, NW
Suite 200
Washington, DC 20036

American Public Welfare
  Association
1125 15th Street, NW
Suite 300
Washington, DC 20005

American Public Works
  Association
1313 East 60th Street
Chicago, IL 60637

American Society for Public
  Administration
1120 G Street, NW
Washington, DC 20005

American Water Works Association
6666 West Quincy Avenue
Denver, CO 80235

Associationof State and Inter-
  state Water Pollution
  Control Administrators
444 North Capitol Street, NW
Room 330
Washington, DC 20001

Building Officials and Code
  Administrators
17926 S. Halsted Street
Homewood, IL 60430

Council for International
  Urban Liaison
818 18th Street, NW
Suite 840
Washington, DC 20006

Council for Urban Economic
  Development
1730 K Street, NW
Suite 1009
Washington, DC 20006

Council of State Community
  Affairs Agencies
444 North Capitol Street
Suite 349
Washington, DC 20001

Council of State Governments
Iron Works Pike
P. O. Box 11910
Lexington, KY 40578

Council of State Housing Agencies
1133 15th Street, NW
Suite 514
Washington, DC 20005

Council of State Planning
Agencies
400 North Capitol Street
Suite 291
Washington, DC 20001

Institute of Transportation
Engineers
525 School Street, SW
Suite 410
Washington, DC 20024

International Association of
Chiefs of Police
13 Firstfield Road
Gaithersburg, MD 20878

International Association of
Fire Chiefs
1329 18th Street, NW
Washington, DC 20036

International City Management
Association
1120 G Street, NW
Suite 300
Washington, DC 20005

International Personnel Management
Association
1850 K Street, NW
Room 870
Washington, DC 20006

International Urban Technology
Exchange Program, Ltd.
250 M Bedford Chambers
Convent Gardens
London, WC2, United Kingdom

Municipal Finance Officers
Association
180 North Michigan Avenue
Suite 800
Chicago, IL 60601

National Academy of Public
Administration
1120 G Street, NW
Washington, DC 20005

National Association of Attorneys
General
444 North Capitol Street
Room 177
Washington, DC 20001

National Association of Housing
& Redevelopment Officials
2600 Virginia Avenue, NW
Room 404
Washington, DC 20037

National Association of Regional
Councils
1700 K Street, NW
13th Floor
Washington, DC 20006

National Association of State
Mental Health Program Dir.
1001 3rd Street, SW
Suite 114
Washington, DC 20024

National Association of Schools of
Public Affairs and Admin.
1120 G Street, NW
Washington, DC 20005

National Association of State
Budget Officers
444 North Capitol Street
Suite 328
Washington, DC 20001

National Association of Tax
Administrators
444 North Capitol Street
Suite 334
Washington, DC 20001

National Association of Towns
and Townships
1522 K Street, NW
Suite 730
Washington, DC 20005

National Institute of Governmental
Purchasing
1735 Jefferson Davis Highway
Suite 101
Arlington, VA 22202

National Institute of Municipal
Law Officers
1000 Connecticut Avenue, NW
Room 800
Washington, DC 20036

National League of Cities
1301 Pennsylvania Avenue, NW
6th Floor
Washington, DC 20004

National Municipal League
47 East 68th Street
New York, NY 10021

National Recreation and Park
Association
3101 Park Center Drive
Arlington, VA 22302

National School Boards Association
1055 Thomas Jefferson Street
Suite 600
Washington, DC 20007

Police Executive Research Forum
1909 K Street, NW
Suite 400
Washington, DC 20006

Public Administraton Service
1497 Chain Bridge Road
McLean, VA 22101

Public Technology, Inc.
1301 Pennsylvania Avenue, NW
8th Floor
Washington, DC 20004

United States Conference of
Mayors
1620 Eye Street, NW
4th Floor
Washington, DC 20006

Water Pollution Control Federation
2626 Pennsylvania Avenue, NW
3rd Floor
Washington, DC 20037

Communities

Center for Community Change
1000 Wisconsin Ave., N.W.
Washington, DC 20007
   Provides advice and information to low-income and minority community based organizations.

International City Management
   Association
1120 G Street, N.W.
Washington, DC 20005
   Provides training, consultation, and technical assistance for city managers and midlevel public administrators.

National Center for Community Action
1328 New York Avenue, N.W.
Washington, DC 20005
   Provides information, training and technical assistance to Community Action Agencies (CAAs).

National League of Cities
1301 Pennsylvania Ave., N.W.
Washington, DC 20004
   Provides information on policy issues of concern to municipal government.

National Training and Information
   Center
1123 W. Wathington Blvd.
Chicago, IL 60637
   This is a non-profit educational institution which works with community groups on neighborhood issues.

National Urban Coalition
1201 Connecticut Ave., N.W.
Washington, D.C. 20036
   This is an urban action, advocacy and information organization which focuses on the needs of business, labor, minorities, and mayors in central cities.

Education

Community Education Skills Exchange
   Network (CESEN)
c/o Program for Community Education
   Development, AOB IV
University of California
Davis, CA 95616
   Shares information, skills and experience among practitioners of community education and development.

Clearinghouse for Community-Based
   Free Standing Educational Institutions.
1806 Vernon Street, N.W.
Washington, DC 20009
   This is an organization of community based educational institutions. Provides information and technical assistance.

Federal Community Education
   Clearinghouse Informatics, Inc.
6000 Executive Blvd.
Rockville, MD 20852
   Provides community educators with specific material relevant to their needs.

Institute for Responsive Education
704 Commonwealth Ave.
Boston, MA 02215
   Assists parent groups and urban minorities on issues of participation in decision-making.

National Alternative Schools Program
c/o School of Education
University of Massachusetts
Amherst, MA 01003
   Serves as a clearinghouse for information on alternative public schools.

99

National Coalition of Alternative
   Community Schools
c/o The Alternative Schools Network
2044 West Grenshaw
Chicago, IL 60612

National Committee for Citizens
   in Education (N.C.C.E.)
410 Wilde Lake Village Green
Columbia, MD 21044
   Provides assistance primarily to parent leaders.

U.S. Department of Education
400 Maryland Ave., S.W.
Washington, D.C. 20202

Health

Alternative Medical Association
7915 S.E. Stark Street
Portland, OR 97215
   Collects and disseminates information relating to holistic health and
   natural therapeutic techniques.

American Medical Association
535 N. Dearborn Street
Chicago, Il 60610
   Provides information on medical
   practices and disease control.

American Nurses Association, Inc.
2420 Pershing Rd.
Kansas City, MO 64108
   Provides information on nursing and
   rehabilitation practices and services.

National Health Council, Inc.
70 West 40th St.
New York, NY 10018
   Provides information on health policies and programs and career opportunities.

National Association of Community
   Health Centers, Inc. (NACHC)
1625 I Street, N.W.
Suite 420
Washington, DC 20006
   Offers a broad range of programs
   designed to promote community
   health center development.

U.S. Department of Health and
   Human Services
Public Health Service
200 Independence Ave., S.W.
Washinggton, DC 20201

Mental Health and Substance Abuse

Alcoholics Anonymous
P.O. Box 459
Grand Central Station
New York, NY 10017

American Psychiatric Association
1400 K Street, N.W.
Washington, DC 20005

American Psychological Association
1200 17th Street, N.W.
Washington, D.C. 20037

Drug Education Program
Center for Older Adults
5820 Germantown Ave.
Philadelphia, PA 19144

Drug Information Center
1763 Moss Street
Eugene, OR 97403

Family Service Association of America
44 East 23rd Street
New York, NY 10010

National Association of Social Workers
7981 Eastern Ave.
Silver Spring, MD 20910

National Council on Alcoholism
733 3rd Ave.
New York, NY 10017

Recovery, Inc.
116 South Michigan Ave.
Chicago, IL 60603

Seniors

American Association of Retired
  Persons
1909 K Street, N.W.
Washington, DC 20049

Center for Older Adults
5820 Germantown Ave.
Philadelphia, PA 19144

Gray Panthers
3635 Chestnut Street
Philadelphia, PA 19104

National Council of Senior Citizens
925 15 St., N.W.
Washington, D.C. 20005

National Council on the Aging
600 Maryland Ave., S.W.
Washington, D.C. 20024

Youth

Association for the Care of Children's
  Health
3615 Wisconsin Ave., N.W.
Washington, DC 20016

Association for Childhood Education
3615 Wisconsin Avenue
Washington, DC 20016

Child Study Association of America
67 Irving Place
New York, NY 10003

Carnegie Council on Children
437 Madison Avenue
New York, NY 10022

Massachusetts Committee for Children
  and Youth
14 Beacon Street, Suite 706
Boston, MA 02108

National Association for Retarded
  Children, Inc.
2709 Avenue East
Arlington, TX 76011

National Center for Prevention and
  treatment of Child Abuse and
  Neglect
1205 Oneida Street
Denver, CO 80220

National Network of Runaway and
  Youth Services
1705 De Sales Street, N.W.
Washington, DC 20036

Office of Services for Children
  and Youth
Department of Health and Human
  Services
200 Independence Ave., S.W.
Washington, DC 20201

Volunteers

ACTION
806 Connecticut Avenue, N.W.
Washington, DC 20525
    this is a federal agency which ad-
    ministers a wide range of volunteer
    programs from Foster Grandparents
    to the Peace Corps.

Association of Volunteer Bureaus
P.O. Box 125
801 North Fairfax Street
Alexandria, VA 22314
    Provides consultation to agencies and
    community groups on volunteer-
    ism.

National Center for Voluntary Action
1111 N. 19th Street
Arlington, VA 22207
    Serves as a clearinghouse on all aspects of volunteer service programming.

National Information Center on
    Volunteerism, Inc.
1540 30th Street
Boulder, CO 80302
    Assists volunteer activities related to criminal justice programs.

United Way of America
99 Park Ave.
New York, NY 10017

APPENDIX C: SEARCH SERVICES

On request, services listed below will scan the literature on any subject and will retrieve abstracts, bibliographic references and other forms of specialty information.

ERIC (Educational Resources Information Center)
National Institute of Education
U.S. Department of Education
Washington, DC 20208

This is a nationwide information system which acquires, abstracts, indices, and disseminates materials on many aspects of education. ERIC consists of a coordinating staff in Washington, D.C. and sixteen Clearinghouses located at universities or professional organizations around the country.

HSIC (Human Service Information Center)
1602 17th Street, N.W.
Washington, DC 20006

Monitors federal legislation and program issues as related to human services.

National Center for Education Statistics
Statistical Information Office
Presidential Building, Room 205
400 Maryland Avenue, S.W.
Washington, DC 20202

Publishes reports and conducts studies that provide data to assist decision makers in forming educational policies.

National Clearinghouse for Drug Abuse Information
P.O. Box 416
Kensington, MD 20795

This is the information center of the National Institute on Drug Abuse. Provides research services and professional journals, fact sheets, manuals and guides on drug abuse issues.

National Clearinghouse for Alcoholic Information
P.O. Box 2345
Rockville, MD 20852

This is the information center of the National Institute on Alcohol Abuse and Alcoholism. It collects and disseminates information pertaining to prevention, treatment, and research aspects of alcohol abuse and alcoholism.

National Clearinghouse for Mental Health Information
Public Inquiries Section
5600 Fishers Lane
Rockville, MD 20857

This is a national center for the collection, storage, retrieval and dissemination of scientific information in the area of mental health. It is a subdivision of the National Institute of Mental Health.

NTIS (National Technical Information Service)
U.S. Department of Commerce
5285 Port Royal Road
Springfield, VA 22161

NTIS is the central source for the public sale of U.S. Government sponsored research, foreign technical reports and other analyses prepared by national and local government agencies, their contractors, and grantees. It is one of the world's leading processors of specialty information.

Project SHARE
P.O. Box 2309
Rockville, MD 20852

Project SHARE Human Services Bibliography Series contains selected abstracts of documents that are related to specific subjects in Human Services.

SCANN-CFF (Service Center for Aging Information — Central Control Facility)
Inter America Research Associates, Inc.
155 Wilson Blvd., Suite 600
Rosslyn, VA 22209

SCANN utilizes an information storage and retrieval system for the collection and dissemination of information on aging. Data bases are: bibliographic, thesaurus, experience exchange, U.S. Administration on Aging and federally funded research projects.

CHILD CUSTODY SERVICES PROGRAM, CITY OF ATLANTIC SHORES*

I. *EXECUTIVE SUMMARY*

A. Introduction

This report is sponsored by the Court Services Unit of the City of Atlantic Shores, Virginia. The project team was comprised of one outside consultant, and two inside members of the CSU working in close consultation with other staff members of the CSU. The program design analysis was begun in January of 1983 and completed in June of 1983 and utilized 0.6 person years of effort. The purpose of this report is to identify alternative methods of resolving child custody cases in the Juvenile and Circuit Courts and to recommend an approach that is likely to be more cost-effective than present procedures.

This report is divided into two sections. The first section, called the Executive Summary, contains a statement of the problem, a description of the present program, and a recommendation for dealing with the problem. The second section called the Management Report, contains detailed descriptions of the alternatives that were identified including costs, effectiveness and feasibility information, and a final recommendation along with supporting rationale. A preliminary view of how to implement the recommended alternative is also presented.

B. Problem Statement

As the divorce rate continues to escalate, there is the growing problem of deciding custodial rights—namely, which parent should have the child and the time and manner of parental visitations. It is questionable that the present legal approach to custodial disputes serves the best interests of either the child or the parents as measured by the growing number of cases that are relitigated.

A recent study of randomly selected cases reveals that in cases that involve minor children, relitigation is a common occurrence. Fifty-two percent of the divorced parents were back in court inside of two years; and a majority of these couples had anywhere from two to ten court appearances. This compares to divorced couples without children where only one in twenty return to court to enforce or modify the original decree.

There are a number of reasons which help to explain why custody cases are difficult to resolve. In many instances, hostility between divorcing parents significantly constrains mutual agreement on who should have the child. More important is the fact that the courts have no clear guidelines in resolving custody disputes. Courts are instructed to award custody according to the "best interests of the child," but because of its vagueness, it is a virtually useless test in most cases. Deciding what is best for the child requires careful diagnosis and prescription which is beyond the traditional adversarial procedures of the courtroom. Consequently, the number of repeat cases in the

---

*This program was designed and written by Andrew Harmond.

Atlantic Shores civil court system have increased by 50% over a five year period from 1976 to 1981. This has served to overload the courts. In addition, counseling professionals testify to the increased stress on parents and children that result from the present system of resolving custodial disputes.

C. Program Description

The court Services Unit was established in February, 1976 to conduct investigations of families involved in custodial disputes. These investigations entail writing reports with recommendations to be submitted to the Juvenile or Circuit Courts. The recommendations usually represent the primary means by which a judge determines which parent is unfit for custody. This process is designed to meet the following CSU goal and objectives:

Goal: To establish and maintain effective methods of resolving child custody dispute cases as will best meet the needs of the child, divorcing parents, and the court of jurisdiction.
Objectives:
(1) Reduce the rate of relitigation in child custody dispute cases;
(2) Provide more expeditious processing of child custody cases;
(3) Secure an agreement that is in the best interests of the child;
(4) Increase the individual coping skills of the litigating parents.

Evidence that shortcomings exist in the current program was detected by the CSU staff. Though substantial amounts of time and effort are spent on investigations, in many instances they fall short of addressing the unique needs of particular families. Relitigation has been increasing and, according to CSU staff, "the high level of dysfunction manifested by these families, especially the destructive impact on children, has evidenced the need for a greater therapeutic focus." Consequently, failure to meet these needs suggests that an alternative approach be found.

D. Methodology

The process by which program alternatives were generated is as follows:
Step 1—The project team became familiar with the stated goals and objectives of the CSU. This was accomplished through a review of program documents and brainstorming with the CSU staff.
Step 2—A search for alternative approaches was conducted utilizing the following sources: agency personnel, court personnel, journal articles, community-based organizations such as lawyer associations and mediation foundations, and social service agencies that deal with custody and visitation issues.
Step 3—Alternatives were described as to procedures, required resources, and advantages and disadvantages.
Step 4—An alternative was selected from a final listing of three as based on a comparison of estimated cost, effectiveness and feasibility data.

E. Recommendations

The introduction of a mediation/counseling component into the operations of the CSU shows the greatest promise of achieving program goals and objectives. In this approach, the CSU would offer individual and family therapy sessions to all families referred to the program by the Juvenile and Circuit Courts. Through mediation services, moreover, program staff members would assist parents in resolving custody and visitation disputes. It is expected that the rate of relitigation is likely to decrease under this approach since studies have shown that individuals demonstrate greater adherence to decisions in which they are an active participant.

Implementation of this alternative will require hiring training consultants and then training staff in mediation and counseling skills. The anticipated time-frame for implementation is approximately six months.

II. MANAGEMENT REPORT

A. Methodology

1. *Program Goals and Objectives*

Program goals and objectives were identified through a careful inspection of CSU documentation and several interviews with the program manager and her staff. They are as follows:

Goal: To establish and maintain effective methods of resolving child custody dispute cases as will best meet the needs of the child, divorcing parents, and the court of jurisdiction.

Objectives:

(1) Reduce the rate of relitigation in child custody dispute cases. *Performance criteria:* Percentage reduction in the rate of relitigation, 1984 compared to 1983.

(2) Provide more expeditious processing of child custody cases. *Performance criteria:* Reduction in the average amount of days it takes to settle a custody case, 1984 compared to 1983; reduction in pending caseload, 1984 compared to 1983.

(3) Secure an agreement that is in the best interests of the child. *Performance criteria:* Child's sense of well being—percentage good, moderate, low, 1984 compared to 1983.

(4) Increase the individual coping skills of litigating parents. *Performance criteria:* Percentage of clients that sustain agreements, 1984 compared to 1983; percentage of clients who report satisfactory adjustment, 1984 compared to 1983.

2. *Program Alternatives*

ALTERNATIVE A: Custody Investigations Extended at a Higher Level of Effort

Description. This alternative would extend the present program at a higher level of effort through the addition of one investigator to the staff of the CSU for a total of five investigators. CSU workload projections show a growing case load as a result of increasing litigation in child custody cases. To deal with this, an additional investigator will provide improved coverage and consequently more careful investigations and fact finding to guide the court. In addition, this approach addresses the problem of relitigation and family stress indirectly by providing the courts with better information so that custody decisions may reflect the best interests of all concerned.

Procedural Details. Upon being referred to the CSU by the court, an investigator will contact the involved parties to set up an initial meeting. During this session, the investigator obtains background information on both the parents and the children whose custody is being disputed. This information is then used to begin a more thorough search of the litigants' backgrounds. By extending interviews to neighbors, relatives, and business associates, additional information can be collected. A report is completed and communicated to the court of jurisdiction.

Advantages

—Provides more detailed case information on which the courts can base a decision.

—Helps meet the expanding case load needs of the CSU.

—The greater level of effort will help to reduce the amount of time it takes to complete an investigation which is sometimes as long as a year.

Disadvantages

—This alternative does not deal with the targeted need to increase the coping skills of parents or children involved in custody disputes.

—More detailed and intensive investigations, as proposed here, may be viewed as an invasion of privacy by clients.

—This alternative will be more costly than the present program.

—Clients are likely to complain about the lack of information feedback during the course of the investigation which would still extend over many months in most cases.

Recommendation. Based on the analysis performed, this alternative is considered secondary. Should unforeseen problems hamper implementation of the recommended alternative, this approach could serve as backup.

ALTERNATIVE B: Mediation/Counseling

Description. This alternative introduces a mediation/counseling component into the operations of the CSU. The CSU would offer individual and conjoint therapy sessions to all families referred to the program by the Juvenile and Circuit Courts. This should help divorcing families to better cope with stress. In addition, by introducing mediation into CSU services, program staff will be able to assist parents and children to resolve custody and visitation disputes. It is expected that as a result of these measures, the rate of relitigation will decrease since studies have shown that individuals demonstrate greater adherence to decisions in which they are an active participant.

To be effective, mediation/counseling services would require cooperation between the courts, the CSU staff, and the Atlantic Shores Department of Social Services. However, no additional resources would be required after the first year of training. Since all CSU personnel currently have mediation/counseling skills, the amount of required training will be minimal—approximately 4 hours a week for two months. Adoption of this alternative would also increase the current range of services at the same time that the CSU staff address the targeted problems of excessive relitigation and family dysfunction.

Procedural Details. Upon being referred to the CSU by the court, all parties including the natural parents, disputed children, step-parents, or involved relatives will be convened as a group at an initial meeting. At this time, the role of the CSU will be explained and the parties will be given the option of participating in mediation/counseling sessions or selecting the more traditional investigatory approach. If they opt for the latter, they may still request mediation/counseling at any time during the investigation. Where they agree to mediation/counseling at the very beginning, they next negotiate a "contract" which sets the schedule for further sessions.

In preparing for such sessions, the counselor must initially diagnose the nature of the custody problem and determine whether custody actions were initiated primarily because of hostility between divorcing parents. Counseling will be based on conjoint meetings aimed at reaching a workable agreement which everyone can agree is in the best interest of the disputed children. Community resources will be identified and established for the continuing support of family members. If a settlement is reached, a written statement will be prepared, reviewed, and signed by the petitioners. This custody/visitation agreement may then be submitted to the court as the disposition of litigation. If the disputants are unable to reach an agreement, an investigation will then be conducted and a report will be submitted to the court.

Advantages

—Provides a more open, flexible and participatory approach to the resolution of family custody disputes.

—Attempts to strengthen family coping skills.

—Increases the range of services being delivered.

—Additional resource requirements are minimal.

—The courts and other participating administrative agencies are supportive.

Disadvantages

—Lawyers are likely to view mediation/counseling in divorce proceedings as being detrimental to their professional interests. Some opposition is likely.

—Mediation/counseling is not likely to work well in situations where participants lack mutual respect and where multiple areas of disagreement exist.

Recommendation. Based on the analysis performed, this alternative is given highest priority and recommended as the most feasible way to address the problem of increasing relitigation in the courts and the stress of parents and children in custody dispute cases.

ALTERNATIVE C: Arbitration

Description. This alternative involves the elimination of the CSU as it now exists and the introduction of an arbitration unit to deal with custody conflicts. The Atlantic Shores Department of Social Services in consultation with the Juvenile and Circuit Courts would contract with the American Arbitration Association (AAA) to provide arbitration services in custody cases. In utilizing this approach, the contending parties would submit their positions to a third party who tailors a resolution based on the issues in dispute. Unlike a mediator's role, recommendations that are formulated through arbitration are generally non-negotiable and binding on the parties. However, the decision can be appealed to the civil courts after a waiting period. It is expected that this approach would lighten the courts' child custody caseload and possibly reduce the rate of repeat cases.

Implementation of this alternative would require funds to contract out. In addition, first year program costs would include the salaries of current members of the CSU to allow time for their relocation to other agencies. Service levels are expected to increase as studies have shown that arbitration takes less time and is more expeditious than litigation.

Procedural Details. Upon application to the court, the divorcing family would be referred to the AAA. A local office would be established in the city of Atlantic Shores. Under this system, the arbitrator would arrange an initial meeting to clarify procedures and to confirm that the arbitration decision shall be legally binding. In subsequent meetings, the arbitrator acts much like a judge taking testimony, hearing witnesses and listening to the arguments of the contending parties. Finally, based on the information presented in these hearings, the arbitrator will render a decision. This decision must be approved by the court of jurisdiction.

Advantages

—This alternative would provide greater convenience as to time and place compared to the present program.

—The adversarial courtroom atmosphere would be avoided.

—Services would be delivered more expeditiously than is presently the case.

—Arbitration should result in a slight decline in the rate of relitigation of custody cases.

Disadvantages

—The Code of Virginia would have to be modified to allow arbitration in custody cases.

—The legal profession is likely to be opposed.

—Starting-up costs during the first year would be high.

—Clientele trust in this process is an unknown factor.

—Some interruption of service during transition period.

Recommendation. Based on the analysis performed, this alternative is rejected as being both economically and politically infeasible.

3. *Estimating Costs, Effectiveness and Feasibility*

During the past five years, the number of first-time custody cases brought before the courts had increased from 500 to 700. It is expected that the number of custody cases will increase by 250 over the next five years (1983 to 1988). As caseload rises, so, too, does the number of cases being relitigated. Having determined this, costs for each alternative being considered were then estimated on the basis of resources that would be needed to meet the rising service demand. In making such estimates, fixed and variable costs were distinguished for each alternative. Alternative A and B did not pose any significant difficulties since most of the costs for personnel and facilities could be carried over from the present program to the new program. However, Alternative C would require contracting out in addition to utilizing old personnel during the first year. This would increase first-year costs appreciably by estimating partial costs for AAA in addition to CSU staff salaries.

Effectiveness estimates are based on the judgement of a panel of experts who responded to specific questions on such matters as relitigation, court caseload, coping skills of the parents, and the needs and interests of the children. In addition, comparable programs in other parts of the country were reviewed to discern likely effectiveness as based on reports and evaluations. This included studies of Santa Clara and Los Angeles counties in California, Hennepin County, Minnesota, and Camden County, New Jersey as being the most useful.

4. *Data Summaries*

TABLE 1: COST COMPARISONS

	Alternative	A	B	C
	Personnel	130,000	110,000	110,000
1st	Other Personnel Costs	24,700	20,900	20,900
Year	Non Personnel Costs	15,900	15,386	15,386
Cost	Other Expenditures	—	3,000	65,000
	TOTAL	170,600	149,286	211,286

TABLE 1: COST COMPARISONS (Cont'd)

	Alternative	A	B	C
	Personnel	136,000	115,000	—
2nd	Other Personnel Costs	25,840	21,850	5,700
Year	Non Personnel Costs	16,200	15,690	—
Cost	Other Expenditures	—	—	150,000
	TOTAL	178,040	152,540	155,700
	GRAND TOTAL	348,640	301,826	366,986

TABLE 2: EFFECTIVENESS COMPARISONS*

Criteria	Alternative A	Alternative B	Alternative C
A 10% reduction in cases relitigated, 1984 compared to 1983	+	+ +	+
A 20% reduction in the average number of days required to settle a custody case, 1984 compared to 1983	+ +	+	+ +
A 20% reduction in pending caseload, 1984 compared to 1983	+ +	+	+ +
Child's sense of well-being—50% reporting moderate or good	−	+ +	−
Coping skills—10% increase in clients sustaining custody settlement, 1984 compared to 1983	−	+ +	−
Coping skills—10% increase in clients who report satisfactory adjustment, 1984 compared to 1983	−	+ +	−

*Scoring is as follows:
+ + = effective impact
+ = some impact
− = no impact

B. Recommendations

Alternative B—mediation and counseling—shows the greatest promise of achieving the program goals and objectives of the Court Services Unit and is rated highest of the three alternatives that have been analyzed. Adoption of this alternative would have the full support of the CSU staff, the courts, and the clientele being served. In addition, it poses only minimal risk of service disruption during the start-up phase. The only foreseeable impediment to adoption may be the special interests of affected attorneys. There is indication, however, that most attorneys are aware of the performance gaps of the present adversarial system and are willing to adjust to proposals for improving the system. In addition, this alternative allows the CSU staff to carry out their duties in a more effective manner without having to increase their budget allotments.

Alternative A, which would extend custody investigatons at a higher level of effort, does not directly address the problem of growing relitigation of custody cases;

nor does it directly address the problem of stress on parents and children. Similarly, Alternative C—arbitration—does not deal directly with the problems of relitigation and family stress. Furthermore, starting-up costs during the first year would be high and it does not appear to be very feasible. It is recommended, therefore, that Alternative A be considered as a secondary alternative and Alternative C be rejected.

C. Implementation

Should the proposed program alternative for mediation/counseling be adopted, an implementation team should be appointed to oversee an implementation workplan, coordinate implementation activities and monitor the progress of implementation.

It is suggested that the implementation team be composed of the same two agency persons and outside consultant who were involved with guiding the program design project. The Executive Director of CSU has the background and experience to coordinate organizational operations and manage resources while the program analyst would be responsible for monitoring progress. In addition, a CSU staff member would perform a general support role. The implementation team should work with the mediation/counseling program until it is established within the CSU. It is expected that within approximately six months, the team would be dissolved and the program would continue as a routine service of the CSU. A proposed workplan follows.

1. *Implementation Schedule*

Tasks	July	Aug.	Sep.	Oct.	Nov.	Dec
Establish implementation team	—					
Orient CSU staff		—				
Hire training consultant		—				
Establish external liaison (courts, social services, bar, community support groups)		—	—	—		
Staff training			—	—		
Monitor	—	—	—	—	—	
Assessment and written report						—

2. *Monitoring Implementation*

When implementation begins, the implementation team will monitor how the program is progressing. In performing this role, the team will utilize the schedule for determining whether tasks are proceeding according to schedule. In addition, program operations, resources and organizational factors will also be accounted for. In monitoring program operations, data will be collected to assess the quality of mediation/counseling services and how they are impacting clients. On questions of resources, it must be determined whether counselors have the appropriate skills and whether funding and facilities are adequate for the planned processing of custody cases. Organizational factors will be observed to determine bottlenecks and sources of opposition.

Information on these factors will be generated from examination of available records, recorded observations of operations, and periodic surveys of clients. Where appropriate, the implementation team will provide feedback to the program staff to correct deficiencies.

GLOSSARY _____

Alternative: A possible course of action that may contribute to the attainment of goals and objectives and the resolution of a public problem.

Change Agent: Any individual or group operating to change the status quo.

Change Object: Any idea, technology or method which modifies the existing way of doing something.

Cost-Benefit Analysis: A study of the relationships between costs and outputs of programs, usually expressed in monetary terms.

Effectiveness: A criterion according to which an alternative is recommended if it results in the achievement of a valued outcome or effect.

Efficiency: A criterion according to which an alternative is recommended if it results in a higher ratio of outputs to inputs or costs.

Equity: A criterion according to which an alternative is recommended if it results in a more just or fair distribution of resources in society.

Evaluation: The analytic method used to produce information about the value or worth of past and/or future courses of program action.

Feasibility: The quality of whether a program can be carried out successfully given various possible constraints; particularly political and organizational constraints.

114

Forecasting: The analytic method used to produce information about the probable consequences of future courses of action.

Implementation: The execution and steering of program actions over time.

Incidence: The number of new cases of a particular problem or condition that are identified or arise in a specified area during a specified period of time.

Indicator: A measure reflecting a problem or condition and for which data is available.

Innovation: An idea, technology or method perceived as being new by the unit of adoption.

Intervention: A program or other planned effort designed to produce intended change in a target population or situation.

Issue: A disagreement or conflict among policy actors about an actual or potential course of action.

Monitoring: The analytic method used to produce information about the past and present consequences of policies and programs.

Needs Assessment: A systematic appraisal of the type, depth and scope of a problem as perceived by study targets or service providers.

Opportunity Cost: The benefits sacrificed by investing resources to produce one product when another more profitable investment could have been made.

Outcome: An observed consequence or result of a program action.

Performance Criteria: Standards according to which program action is evaluated.

Performance Gap: A discrepancy between the criteria of satisfaction in performing some act and the actual performance of that act.

Planned Change: A purposive attempt to change the existing way of doing things in an organization.

Policy: A broad statement of goals and objectives.

Prediction: A forecast based on explicit theoretical assumptions.

Prevalence: The number of existing cases with a given condition in a particular area at a specified time.

Program Adoption: An authoritative decision to allocate resources to a program change.

Program Analysis: Estimating the costs, effectiveness and feasibility of different ways of accomplishing a public purpose.

Program Design: A plan which converts goals into objectives, defines relevant target groups, and formulates specific interventions.

Program Goal: An aim or purpose which is broadly stated, formerly defined, unspecified as to time and target groups, and unquantified.

Program Elements: Procedures and organizational arrangements that are defined to deliver services to appropriate target groups or situations.

Program Impact: A change in behavior or in the environment that results from program action.

Program Input: Resources such as time, money, personnel, equipment, or supplies used to produce program outputs.

Program Objective: A specifically defined statement which specifies the desired result or outcome of a program intervention.

Program Output: A good, service, or resource delivered to target groups and beneficiaries.

Program Performance: The degree to which a program activity contributes to the attainment of program goals and objectives.

Public Problem: An unrealized need, value, or opportunity that may be achieved through public action.

Rate: The occurrence or existence of a condition expressed as a proportion of units in the population (e.g., crime reported per 1,000 adults).

Responsiveness: A criterion according to which an alternative is recommended if it results in the satisfaction of the needs, preferences, or values of citizens or clients.

Routinization: The absorption of a program change into established practice so that it is no longer perceived as new or different.

Service Delivery: Organizational arrangements including staff, procedures and activities, physical plants, and materials needed to provide program benefits.

Survey: The systematic collection of information from large study groups, usually by means of interviews or questionnaires administered to a sample of units in the population.

Target Group: Persons, households, or organizations on which a program is expected to have an effect.

ANNOTATED BIBLIOGRAPHY ___

Chapter One

Hatry, Harry, Blair, Louis, Fisk, Donald and Kimmel, Wayne. *Program Analysis for State and Local Governments*. Washington, D.C.: The Urban Institute, 1976.
Shows how program analysis can be used as a management technique for solving complex problems in state and local government. Emphasizes application rather than theory or concepts.

Havelock, Ronald G. *Planning for Innovation Through Dissemination and Utilization of Knowledge*. Ann Arbor, Mich.: Institute for Social Research, the University of Michigan, 1969.
Provides a framework for understanding the processes of innovation, dissemination, and knowledge utilization. Though a little dated, a very good bibliography and a review of the literature are presented.

Lambright, W. Henry. *Technology Transfer to Cities: Processes of Choice at the Local Level*. Boulder, CO.: Westview Press, 1979.
Describes the decision-making process that is involved in introducing innovations to local public organizations. Of special importance is the role of local entrepreneurship and coalition-building in technology transfer.

Public Technology, Inc. *Program Evaluation and Analysis, A Technical Guide for State and Local Governments*. Washington, D.C.: U.S. Department of Housing and Urban Development, November, 1978.
Demonstrates how to do program analysis and evaluation. This work was developed with the assistance of various state and local government officials as potential users.

Yin, Robert K. *Changing Urban Bureaucracies*. Lexington, Mass.: Lexington Books, D.C. Heath, 1979.
Describes the process by which an innovation moves through various "passages" and "cycles" until it is routinized. The analysis is based on case studies of technological innovation in nineteen cities. This study is an important advance in the area of innovation and change in public organizations.

Zaltman, Gerald, and Duncan, Robert. *Strategies for Planned Change*. New York: John Wiley and Sons, 1973.
A compendium of ideas on change processes in organizations. Identifies various strategies that a change agent should be aware of.

Chapter Two

Cleland, David I., and King, William. *Systems Analysis and Project Management*, 3rd ed. New York: McGraw-Hill, 1983.
This book provides an understanding of the basic concepts and procedures involved in planning and managing complex projects. Such projects must take into account the interdependence of the efforts of a variety of people and organizations and the tradeoffs that must be made between the project's time requirement, cost, and performance. An understanding of the skills required for project management should prove quite valuable to members of the project team.

Rosenbaum, Robert A. *The Public Issues Handbook, A Guide for the Concerned Citizen*. Westport, Conn.: Greenwood Press, 1983.
Defines twenty-four public issues in the United States and provides supporting data and bibliographies. This work is very useful for those persons who are either searching for or wanting to know more about a problem area.

Chapter Three

Bennis, Warren G., Benne, Kenneth D., and Chin, Robert, eds. *The Planning of Change*. New York: Holt, 1969.
The focus of this work is on how change is created, implemented and maintained. Emphasizes the role of the change agent in working with clients and other change agents.

Downs, Anthony. *Inside Bureaucracy*. Boston: Little Brown and Company, 1967.
This book is a classic on the structure and processes of bureaucratic organizations. Writing as a political economist, the author deduces how agencies and bureaucrats are likely to behave in the pursuit of goals. Many good insights on factors that influence change.

National Institute of Mental Health. *A Typological Approach to Do Social Area Analysis*. Department of Health, Education and Welfare, publication Number (ADM) 76–262. Washington, D.C.: U.S. Government Printing Office, 1975.
Demonstrates the use of demographic and similar types of data derived from public records for determining community needs.

Neuber, Keith A., Atkins, William T., Jacobson, James A., and Reuterman, Nicholas A. *Needs Assessment, A Model for Community Planning*. Beverly Hills: Sage Publications, 1980.
Gives step-by-step directions for conducting a needs assessment covering inter-

view procedures, collecting and analyzing data, and making use of the findings within agencies and in the context of broader community planning efforts.

Rothman, Jack, Erlich, John L., Teresa, Joseph G. *Changing Organizations and Community Programs*. Beverly Hills: Sage Publications, 1981.

The authors focus on intervention strategies for influencing social service organizations and solving community welfare problems. Very useful for administrators involved in program change.

Tornatzky, Louis G., Fergus, Esther O., Avellar, Joseph W., Fairweather, George W., with Fleisder, Michael. *Innovation and Social Process, A National Experiment in Implementing Social Technology*. New York: Pergamon Press, 1980.

Through experimental research design, the authors identify intervention strategies that facilitate innovation in a mental health organizational setting. Peer-to-peer interaction, networking, participatory decision-making and other group techniques are analyzed and discussed.

Chapter Four

Bardach, Eugene. *The Skill Factor in Politics*. Berkeley: University of California Press, 1972.

Examines varieties of political skill in the context of California mental health politics in the mid–1960s. A good primer on the use of political strategies for achieving policy goals.

Coplin, William D., and O'Leary, Michael K. *Everyman's "Prince": A Guide to Understanding Your Political Problems*, 2nd ed. North Scituate, Mass.: Duxbury Press, 1976.

Provides a framework for estimating the probable support or opposition among different interests to policy and program alternatives. Very useful for gauging political feasibility of program change.

Moore, Barbara, H., ed. *the Entrepreneur in Local Government*. Washington, D.C.: International City Management Association, 1983.

Shows how local government managers can be entrepreneurial by creating opportunities for improved services under conditions of resource scarcity. Especially pertinent is a chapter titled "The Organizational Climate for Innovation" by Rosabeth Moss Kanter.

Chapter Five

Delbecq, Andres, L., et al. *Group Techniques for Program Planning: A Guide to Nominal Group and Delphi Processes*. Glenview, Il: Scott, Foresman and Company, 1975.

Describes group techniques for problem-solving in organizations. Questionnaires and other instruments for producing and collecting data serve as useful illustration for anyone engaged in program design.

Quade, E.S. *Analysis for Public Decisions*, 2nd ed. New York: North Holland, Elsevier Science Publishing Co., 1982.

An excellent book which focuses on research models for doing policy analysis. Demonstrates both qualitative and quantitative methodologies and shows how they can be used in case studies.

Zaltman, Gerald, and Duncan, Robert. *Strategies for Planned Change*. New York: John Wiley and Sons, 1977.

Chapter 2 on "Defining Social Problems" is excellent and highly recommended as a guide for the change agent or analyst in diagnosing a situation. Presents techniques for gathering problem-related data.

Chapter Six

Hatry, Harry P., Blair, Louis H., Fisk, Donald M., Greiver, John M., Hall, Jr., John R., and Schaenman, Philip S. *How Effective Are Your Community Services?* Washington, D.C.: The Urban Institute and the International City Management Association, 1977.
This manual demonstrates performance measurement and data collection as based on program goals and objectives. Different service areas are illustrated such as transportation, criminal justice, sanitation, solid waste and recreation.

Mager, Robert F. *Goal Analysis*, 1970; and *Preparing Instructional Objectives*, 2nd ed. Belmount, Cal.: Fearon Pitman, 1975.
Never out of date, Robert Mager's books are fun to read. Most important, they help decision makers and analysts discover where they want to go and how they should write it out. Practice exercises are provided.

Chapter Seven

Amara, R.C. "Forecasting From Conjectural Art Toward Science," *The Futurist*, 6, No. 3 (June 1972).
This article examines the conceptual issues of design and measurement in forecasting. Reviews approaches used by the Institute of the Future.

Ascher, William. *Forecasting, An Appraisal for Policy Makers and Planners*. Baltimore: Johns Hopkins University Press, 1978.
Appraises forecasting accuracy in such areas as population, economic growth, transportation, energy and technology. The author sorts out various constraints on accurate forecasting and provides insights on how to improve forecasting methods.

Coke, James G., and Moore, Carl M. *Guide for Leader Using Nominal Group Technique*. Columbus, Ohio: Academy for Contemporary Problems, 1979.
A very useful guide for using Nominal Group Technique. This approach involves an outside facilitator who assists the group in identifying solutions to a clearly defined problem.

Delbecq, Andres, L., Van de Ven, Andrew H., and Gustafson, David H. *Group Techniques for Program Planning: A Guide to Nominal Group and Delphi Processes*. Glenview, Il.: Scott, Foresman and Company, 1975.
See description above.

Kahn, Herman. "The Alternatives Futures Approach" in *Search for Alternatives: Public Policy and the Study of the Future*, Tugwell, F., ed. Cambridge, Mass.: Winthrop Publishers, 1973.
Kahn's article discusses the strengths and weaknesses of the scenario method of forecasting. Other articles in the collection provide excellent descriptions of various futuristic methodologies.

Parnes, Sidney J. "Do You Really Understand Brainstorming?" in Parnes, Sidney J., and Harding, Harold F., eds. *A Source Book for Creative Thinking*. New York: Charles Scribner's Sons, 1962.
Parnes examines the pros and cons of group brainstorming for problem-solving and makes suggestions on how to achieve the best results. This whole volume is recommended for what it says about incorporating creative thinking in the search for effective solutions.

Chapter Eight

Anderson, Lee G. *Benefit-Cost Analysis*. Lexington, Mass.: Lexington Books, 1977.
Treats both the theory and the application of benefit-cost analysis. Useful for those persons seeking an introduction to this form of analysis.

Blalock, Hubert M. *Social Statistics*. New York: McGraw-Hill, 1972.
A basic textbook on the use of statistics in developing programs, making statistics understandable for the beginner.

Coplin, William D., and O'Leary, Michael K. *Everyman's "Prince": A Guide to Understanding Your Political Problems*, 2nd ed. North Scituate, Mass.: Duxbury Press, 1976.
See description above.

Durham, T.R. *An Introduction to Benefit-Cost Analysis for Evaluating Public Programs*. Croton-on-Hudson, N.Y.: Policy Studies Associates, 1977.
This work introduces the basic concepts and techniques employed in benefit-cost studies so that the reader can begin to apply this form of analysis. Provides exercises to ensure familiarity and application.

Hatry, Harry, Blair, Louis, Fisk, Donald and Kimmel, Wayne, *Program Analysis for State and Local Governments*. Washington, D.C.: The Urban Institute, 1976.
Chapter Four and Five present excellent discussion and illustrations on estimating program costs and effectiveness.

Lynch, Thomas D. *Public Budgeting in America*. Englewood Cliffs, N.J.: Prentice-Hall, Inc., 1985.
This text covers all aspects of the budgeting process including preparation. A section on budgeting and program analysis makes for useful background reading.

Rossi, Peter H., and Freeman, Howard E. *Evaluation, A Systematic Approach*, 2nd ed. Beverly Hills: Sage Publications, 1982.
Chapter Three discusses methods of estimating the target population to be served by a program.

Chapter Nine

Hamburg, Morris. *Statistical Analysis for Decision Making*. New York: Harcourt, Brace, 1970.
Shows how to use numbers, graphs, charts, etc. for organizing and presenting data.

Quade, E.S. *Analysis for Public Decisions*, 2nd ed. New York: North Holland, Elsevier Science Publishing Co., 1982.
Presents many good case studies and illustrations on the organization of data for comparing program alternatives.

Chapter Ten

Allen, Richard K. *Organizational Management Through Communications*. New York: Harper & Row, 1977.
The thesis of this book is that legal and social factors are creating ever greater need for effective communication in organizations. The last section deals with "The Manager as a Communication Strategist."

Houp, Kenneth W., and Pearsall, Thomas E. *Reporting Technical Information*, 5th ed. New York: Macmillan Publishing Co., 1984.
Covers all aspects of report writing from selecting a topic to analyzing your audience to methods of organization and exposition.

Rogers, Everett M., and Agaruala-Rogers, Rehka. *Communications in Organizations*. New York: The Free Press, 1976.
Presents a very good overview of the field of organizational communication. Includes an accounting of organizational barriers to communication and how to overcome them.

Strunk, Jr., William, and White, E.B. *The Elements of Style*, 3d ed. New York: Macmillan Publishing Co., 1979.
This is a good technical guide on English usage and composition.

Wilensky, Harold L. *Organizational Intelligence: Knowledge and Policy in Government and Industry*. New York: Basic Books, Inc., 1967.
A classic in the field, this book deals with issues related to the collecting, processing, interpreting, and transmiting of information necessary for effective decision making.

Chapter Eleven

Morris, Lynn Lyons, and Fitz-Gibbon, Carol Taylor. *How to Measure Program Implementation*. Beverly Hills: Sage Publications, 1978.
As this book shows, a program is not likely to work very well unless there is feedback on how it is being implemented. Various methods for measuring implementation are presented.

Nakamura, Robert T., and Smallwood, Frank. *The Politics of Policy Implementation*. New York: St. Martin's Press, 1980.
Shows how the implementation of policy is related to the formulation and evaluation of policy—what happens in one stage affects the other stages. Consequently, implementers can have as much of an impact on policy making, as policy makers can have on implementation. This is an important concept for understanding the implementation process.

Pressman, Jeffrey L., and Wildavsky, Aaron. *Implementation*, 2nd ed. Berkeley: University of California Press, 1979.

First published in 1973, this is one of the earliest studies of the politics of implementation and probably one of the best. Explains why it is so difficult to carry out programs as intended.